Mastering the PMP® Exam [Total Prep]

The Official Study Guide 2019

Based on the PMBOK Guide 6th Edition

Mariam A. Azam, MBA, PMP, CSM

Class materials are based on *A Guide to the Project Management Body of Knowledge, (PMBOK® Guide),* Sixth Edition, Project Management Institute Inc., 2017.

"PMP," "PMBOK," "PMI-ACP" and "PMI" are registered trademarks of the Project Management Institute, Inc.

Copyright – January 2019

All rights reserved.

Contents

Introduction: Project Management Framework 9
   Project Roles 10
   Five Process Groups: 10
   Ten Knowledge Areas: 11
   49 Processes: 11
      Tools and Techniques 13
   Common Inputs 13
   Common Tools and Techniques 14
   Common Outputs 14
   Additional Techniques 15
      Data Gathering 15
      Data Analysis Techniques 17
      Data Representation 22
      Decision Making Techniques 23
      Communication Skills 25
      Interpersonal & Team Skills 25
Project Environments 27
   Organizational Types 27
   Project Management Office (PMO) 29
Role of the Project Manager 30
   Technical Skills 31
   Strategic and Business Management Skills 31
   Leadership Skills 31
   Project Manager Power 31
   Project Manager's Leadership 33
   Project Manager's Personalities 34
Initiating Process Group 35
Key Terms: 38
   Integration Management 38
   Stakeholder Management 38
Planning Process Group 39

Integration Management	53
Scope Management	53
Schedule Management	54
Cost Management	58
Cost Types:	59
Quality Management:	61
Resource Management:	62
Procurement Management:	62
Risk Management:	63
Risk Tools:	65
Executing Process Group	66
Integration Management	74
Resource Management	74
Procurement Management	74
Monitoring and Controlling Process Group	74
Integration Management	82
Scope Management	83
Cost Management	83
Quality Management	83
Procurement Management	85
Closing	86
Integration Management	87
Earned Value Management Formulas	89
PMP® Workbook	95
Introduction	97
Matching	97
Fill in the Blanks	97
Memorization	98
Matching	99
Crossword Puzzles	101
Fill in the Blanks	102
Multiple Choice Questions	103
Project Management Roles and Responsibilities	107
Fill-in the Blanks	107
Matching	109

Initiating	110
Matching	110
Questions	111
Planning	115
Matching	115
Matching	115
Fill-in the Blanks	117
Fill-in the blanks	118
Questions	119
Fill in the Story	121
Put in Order	125
Matching	126
Questions	127
Executing	131
Matching	131
Fill in the Story	131
Questions	135
Monitoring & Controlling	139
Matching	139
Fill in the story	142
Questions	145
Closing	149
Fill-in the Story	149
Questions	149
Earned Value Management	153
Critical Path Exercise	157
Process Matrix Exercise	158
PMP® Workbook Answers	161
Introduction	163
Matching	163
Fill in the Blanks	163
Memorization	163
Matching	164
Crossword Puzzles	164

  Across 164
  Down 164
 Fill in the Blanks 165
 Multiple Choice Questions 165
Project Management Roles and Responsibilities 167
 Fill-in the Blanks 167
 Matching 167
Initiating 168
 Matching 168
 Questions 168
Planning 171
 Matching 171
 Matching 171
 Fill-in the Blanks 171
 Fill-in the blanks 172
 Questions 172
 Fill in the Story 173
 Put in Order 175
 Matching 175
 Questions 176
Executing 177
 Matching 177
 Fill in the Story 177
 Questions 179
Monitoring & Controlling 181
 Matching 181
 Fill in the story 183
 Questions 183
Closing 185
 Fill in the Story 185
 Questions 185
Earned Value Management 187
Critical Path Exercise 193
Process Matrix Exercise 196

List of Tables

Table 1. Process Matrix 13
Table 2. Sphere of Influence and a Project Managers
 Competencies 30
Table 3. Initiating Process Group ITTO Matrix 37
Table 4. Planning Process Group ITTO Matrix 43
Table 5. Executing Process Group ITTO Matrix 67
Table 6. Monitoring and Controlling Process Group ITTO Matrix 77
Table 7. Closing Process Group ITTO Matrix 89

Dear PMP® and CAPM® Test Taker,

Thank you for your interest in ADV Consultant's Ezpm Training. Taking the PMP® or CAPM® exam lets employers know that you have the knowledge and skills needed to manage critical projects. By using the Mastering the PMP® Exam [Total Prep] official Guide book to prepare for the PMP® and CAPM® exam, you're taking a significant step towards achieving your goals of obtaining and achieving your career goals of becoming a certified project manager.

This book, Mastering the PMP® Exam [Total Prep] official Guide 2019, is designed to help you prepare for and build confidence to do your best on the PMP® or CAPM® exam. It's the only guide of its kind on the market that includes real PMP® and CAPM® exam questions published by ADV Consultants, LLC senior PMP® Instructors.

In 2014, while using other study guides to prepare our students for the PMP® and CAPM® exam, we realized that the market was missing a comprehensive quick reference guide that you could use to recap the entire PMBOK Guide 6th edition and would help you pinpoint precisely the content that would be on the exam.

Today, we have helped more than 500 students pass the PMP® and CAPM® exam and become leaders in the Project Management industry. This guide was used to help our students pass the PMP® and CAPM ®, and we want to pass it on to others.

We are driven to keep improving the Mastering the PMP® Exam [Total Prep] official Guide and help you achieve your goals. We applaud your commitment to educational success, and we know that this book and our online training class www.training.ezpmtraining.com will help you make your personal goals.

We wish you success in all your educational and professional goals in the future.

Sincerely,

Mariam Azam

Mariam A. Azam, MBA, PMP, CSM
President of ADV Consultants
www.advconsultants.com

Introduction

Project Management Framework

- **Project:** A temporary endeavor that produces a unique product, service, or result.
- **Program:** A group of related projects that are managed in a coordinated way to obtain benefits not available if managed individually.
- **Portfolio:** A collection of projects, programs, subsidiary portfolios, and operations managed as a group to achieve the strategic objectives of the organization. Tied to the organization's investment.
- **Project Management:** Application of knowledge, skills, tools, and techniques to project activities that help the project manager meet the project requirements. Enables the project manager to execute the project effectively and efficiently.
- **Project Triggers:** Market demands, customer requests, organizational requirements, technology, legal requirements, government regulations, and social need, etc.
- **Operations:** Ongoing production of goods and/or services (e.g., manufacturing, call center, etc.) that use business processes to ensure customer needs is met.
- **Project Life Cycle:** The series of phases that a project passes through from initiation to closure.
- **Project Phase:** A logical collection of related project activities that culminates in the completion of the deliverables.
- **Phase Gate:** A go/no-go decision at the end of the phase to determine to continue to the next phase, proceed with modification, or to end the program/project.

Project Roles

- **Project Manager (PM):** Responsible for achieving the project objectives with the given resources.
- **Project Sponsor:** Provides financial resources and works with the project manager to minimize unnecessary changes.
- **Program Manager:** Responsible for managing programs.
- **Functional Manager:** Manages and owns the resources in a specific department.
- **Customer/User:** Individuals or organization that will receive the projects, product, service, or result.
- **Performing Organization:** The enterprise whose employees are involved in delivering the project.
- **Project Management Team:** Members directly involved in the PM activities.
- **Project Team Members:** Group executing the project activities to deliver the output.
- **Stakeholder:** Anyone that is positively or negatively affected by the project. Everyone!

Five Process Groups:

- **Initiating:** Consists of two (2) processes that define a new project or a new phase of an existing project at a high level to obtain authorization to start.
- **Planning:** Consists of 24 processes that establish the scope, objectives and define the course of action the team will take to complete the project successfully.
- **Executing:** Consists of ten (10) processes that the project team members complete according to the plan to satisfy the project requirements.
- **Monitoring and Controlling:** Consists of twelve (12) processes that track, review, and regulate the progress and performance of the project against the plan. Identify any changes to the plan and initiate the corresponding changes.
- **Closing:** Consists of a single process to formally complete, close the project, phase, or contract.

Ten Knowledge Areas:

- **Project Integration Management:** Putting the project in a cohesive whole.

- **Project Scope Management:** Ensures the project includes all the work required, and only the work required, to complete the project successfully.

- **Project Schedule Management:** Creating and managing the timely completion of the project.

- **Project Cost Management:** Creating and managing the approved time phase budget.

- **Project Quality Management:** The degree to which the project fulfills requirements.

- **Project Resource Management:** Acquiring and managing the resources needed to complete the project successfully.

- **Project Communications Management:** Ensure timely & appropriate generation collection, distribution, storage, retrieval, & ultimate disposition of project information

- **Project Risk Management:** Working to increase the probability and impact of opportunities on the project (positive events), while decreasing the probability and impact of threats to the project (negative events).

- **Project Procurement Management:** The processes necessary to purchase or acquire products, services or results needed from outside the project team.

- **Project Stakeholder Management:** Identify people, groups or organizations that could impact or be impacted.

49 Processes:

Each process is associated with a knowledge area and process group. Each of the processes has their own inputs, tools and techniques and outputs.

Input – Any item either internal or external to the project, which is required by the process before that process proceeds.

Notes

Tools and Techniques

Tools – Something tangible (e.g., template or software program) used in performing an activity to produce a product or result.

Techniques – A defined systematic procedure employed by a human resource to perform an activity to produce a product or result or deliver a service, and that may employ one or more tools (e.g., meetings, interviews, inspection)

Output – A product, result, or service generated by a process; may be an input to a successor process.

Table 1. Process Matrix

Knowledge Area	I	P	E	MC	C
Integration	1	1	2	2	1
Scope		4		2	
Schedule		5		1	
Cost		3		1	
Quality		1	1	1	
Resource		2	3	1	
Communication		1	1	1	
Risk		5	1	1	
Procurement		1	1	1	
Stakeholder	1	1	1	1	
	2	24	10	12	1

Common Inputs

Project Management Plan – How to guide that describes how the project will be executed, monitored and controlled, and closed.

Project Documents – Project artifacts created and updated in various processes (e.g., risk register, issue log, change log, etc.)

Work Performance Data – Raw data collected during the executing process group to be used later to analyze the performance of the project.

Enterprise Environmental Factors – Any internal or external factors that cane influence a project's success.

Organizational Process Assets – Procedures, guidelines, templates, and lessons learned historical information that an organization has from past projects that can be used for the current project.

Common Tools and Techniques

Expert Judgment – Expertise provided by a group or individual with specialized knowledge or training.

Meetings – Interactive communication tool for the exchange or project information.

Common Outputs

Project Document Updates – Updating project artifacts due to changes from processes.

Project Management Updates – Updating the plan and/or components due to changes approved change via change control.

Change Requests – Includes any scope changes, corrective actions, preventive action, and/or defect repairs resulting from the work in the processes.

Organizational Process Assets Updates – Updated procedures, guidelines, templates, lessons learned, etc.

Work Performance Information – Project progress data that has been analyzed through the monitoring and controlling processes.

Additional Techniques

Data Gathering

Collecting data and information from a variety of sources; there are nine data gathering tools throughout the project management process.

- **Benchmarking** – Comparing actuals or planned products, processes, and practices to those of comparable organizations to identify best practices, generate ideas of improvement, and provide a basis for measuring performance. [*Collect requirements; Plan Quality Management; Plan Stakeholder Engagement*]

- **Brainstorming** – Used in a group environment, led by a facilitator it is a technique to gather ideas in a short period of time. The participants generate ideas and then analyze them. [*Develop Project Charter; Develop Project Management Plan; Collect Requirements; Plan Quality Management; Identify Risks; Identify Stakeholders*]

- **Check Sheets** – Also known as Tally Sheets used for gathering data, organizing facts, and collecting attribute data during inspections. [*Control Quality*]

- **Checklists** – A checklist is a list of steps to be carried out for an activity. The list is made as comprehensive as possible so that this becomes the tool to verify that all the required steps for a quality item is carried out without missing any one of them. [*Develop Project Management Plan; Manage Quality; Control Quality*]

- **Focus Groups** – Bringing together prequalified stakeholders and subject matter experts to learn about their expectations about a proposed product. A trained moderator guides the group through an interactive discussion designed to be conversational instead of a one on one interview. [*Develop Project Charter; Develop Project Management Plan; Collect Requirements*]

- **Interviews** – Talking to stakeholder directly to gather information about a specific product or requirement. [*Develop

Notes

Project Charter; Develop Project Management Plan; Collect Requirements; Plan Quality Management; Identify Risks; Perform Qualitative Risk Analysis; Perform Quantitative Risk Analysis; Plan Risk Responses]

- **Market Research** – Gathering information from different sources like online reviews and conferences to identify the market trend and market capabilities. It refines the procurement objectives of the project management team to leverage the mature technologies, processes and organizations. It also balances the risks that are associated with the vendors who provide the services or materials needed for the project. [*Plan Procurement Management*]

- **Questionnaires and Surveys** – Gather information from stakeholders by sending out written questions. [*Collect requirements; Plan Stakeholder Management*]

- **Statistical Sampling** – Selecting a portion of the population to test, testing the whole population would be time consuming and costly. [*Control Quality*]

Data Analysis Techniques

Used to organize, assess, and evaluate data and information.

- **Alternative Analysis** – Evaluating identified options in order to select the options or approaches to use to execute and perform the work of the project. [*Manage Project Knowledge; Monitor and Control Project Work; Plan Scope Management; Create WBS; Plan Schedule Management; Estimate Activity Durations; Plan Cost Management; Estimate Cost; Manage Quality; Estimate Activity Resources; Control Resources; Monitor Stakeholder Engagement*]

- **Assessment of other Risk Parameters** – Taking into consideration other characteristics of risk in addition to probability and impact when prioritizing individual project risks for further analysis and action. (e.g., urgency, proximity; dormancy; manageability; controllability; detectability; connectivity; strategic impact propinquity). [*Perform Qualitative Risk Analysis*]

- **Assumptions and Constraint Analysis** – Exploring the validity of assumptions and constraints to determine which pose a risk to the project. [*Identify Risks*]

- **Cost of Quality** – Total cost of all efforts to achieve product/service quality. Measures all work to ensure conformance to requirements and all work resulting from nonconformance to requirements. [*Estimate Costs; Plan Quality Management*]

- **Cost Benefit Analysis** – A financial analysis tool used to determine the benefits provided by a project against its costs. [*Manage Project Knowledge; Monitor and Control Project Work; Plan Quality Management; Control Resources; Plan Risk Responses*]

- **Decision Tree Analysis** – Uses Earned Monetary Value analysis internally. A decision tree, as the name suggests, is about making decisions when you're facing multiple options. [*Perform Quantitative Risk Analysis*]

- **Document Analysis** – Evaluating available project documentation to identify lessons learned and knowledge sharing for future projects and organizational assets improvement. [*Close Project or Phase; Collect Requirements; Manage Quality; Identify Risks; Identify Stakeholders*]

- **Earned Value Analysis** – Provides an integrated perspective on scope, schedule, and cost performance. [*Monitor and Control Project Work; Control Schedule; Control Costs; Control Procurements*]

- **Influence Diagrams** – A graphical representation of situations showing casual influences, time ordering of events, and other relationships among variables and outcomes. [*Perform Quantitative Risk Analysis*]

- **Iteration Burndown Chart** – Tracks the work that remains to be completed in the iteration backlog. Used to analyze the variance with respect to an ideal burndown based on the work committed from iteration planning. [*Control Schedule*]

- **Make or Buy Analysis** – A general management technique used to determine whether particular work can be best be accomplished by the project team or must be purchased from outside sources. Budget constrains may influence make-or-buy decisions. [*Plan Procurement Management*]

- **Performance Reviews** – To measure, compare, and analyze schedule performance against the schedule baseline such as actual start and finish dates, percent complete, and remaining duration for work in progress. [*Control Schedule; Control Quality; Control Resources; Control Procurements*]

- **Process Analysis** – Identifying opportunities for process improvements. Also examining problems constraints, and non-value-added activities that occur during a process. [*Manage Quality*]

- **Proposal Evaluation** – Reviewing proposals provided by suppliers to support contract award decisions. [*Conduct Procurement*]

- **Regression Analysis** – Where a series of input variables are examined in relation to their corresponding output results in order to develop a mathematical or statistical relationship. [*Close Project or Phase*]

- **Reserve Analysis** – To determine the essential features and relationships of components in the PMP to establish a reserve for the schedule duration, budget, estimated cost, or funds for a project. [*Estimate Activity Durations; Estimate Cost; Determine Budget; Control Costs; Implement Risk Responses*]

- **Risk Data Quality Assessment** – Evaluate the degree to which data about risks is useful for risk management. [*Perform Qualitative Risk Analysis*]

- **Risk Probability and Impact Assessment** – Considering the likelihood that a specific risk will occur. It considers the potential effect on one or more project objectives such as schedule, cost, quality, or performance. [*Perform Qualitative Risk Analysis*]

- **Root Cause Analysis** – Used to determine the basic underlying reason that causes a variance or a defect or a risk. [*Monitor and Control Project Work; Manage Quality; Control Quality; Identify Risks; Plan Stakeholder Engagement; Monitor Stakeholder Engagement*]

Notes

- **Sensitivity Analysis** – Used to determine which individual project risks or other sources of uncertainty have the most potential impact on project outcomes, by correlating variations in project outcomes with variations in elements of quantitative risk analysis model. [*Perform Quantitative Risk Analysis*]

- **Simulation** – Modeling the combined effect of uncertainties to evaluate their potential impact on objectives. [*Develop Schedule; Perform Quantitative Risk Analysis*]

- **Stakeholder Analysis** – Systematically gathering and analyzing quantitative and qualitative information to determine whose interests should be considered throughout the project. [*Plan Risk Management; Identify Stakeholders; Monitor Stakeholder Engagement*]

- **SWOT Analysis** – Examining the project from each strengths, weaknesses, opportunities, and threats perspectives. [*Identify Risks; Plan Stakeholder Engagement*]

- **Technical Performance Analysis** – Comparing technical accomplishments during project execution to the schedule of technical achievement. [*Control Risks*]

- **Trend Analysis** – Using mathematical models to forecast future outcomes based on historical results. [*Monitor and Control Project Work; Close Project or Phase; Control Scope; Control Schedule; Control Cost; Control Resources; Control Procurements*]

- **Variance Analysis** – Determining the cause and degree of difference between the baseline and actual performance. [*Monitor and Control Project Work; Close Project or Phase; Control Scope; Control Schedule; Control Cost*]

- **'What if?' Scenario Analysis** – Evaluating scenarios in order to predict their effort on project objectives. [*Develop Schedule; Control Schedule*]

Data Representation

Graphical representations or other methods used to convey data and information.

- **Affinity Diagrams** – Classifying large number of ideas into groups for review and analysis. [*Collect Requirements; Manage Quality*]

- **Cause and Effect Diagrams** – Graphical technique that helps the team to group ideas and identifies the causes of a problem. Shows how different variables may be linked to the effect (problem). [*Manage Quality; Control Quality*]

- **Control Charts** – Graphic display of process over time and against control limits. Determine whether a process is stable or has predictable performance. [*Control Quality*]

- **Flowcharts** – Graphical representation of a process. Identify and anticipate process problems. [*Plan Quality Management; Manage Quality*]

- **Hierarchical Charts** – Organizational chart structure can be used to show positions and relationships. (e.g., WBS, OBS, RBS) [*Plan Resource Management*]

- **Histograms** – A vertical bar chart shows how often events occur. Show frequencies of errors or periodic staffing levels. [*Manage Quality; Control Quality*]

- **Logical Data Model** – Visual representation of an organization's data described in business language and independent of any specific technology. Can be used to identify where data integrity or other quality issues can arise. [*Plan Quality Management*]

- **Matrix Diagrams** – Used to perform data analysis within the organizational structure created in a matrix. Showing the strength of relationships between factors, causes, and objectives that exist between the rows and columns that form the matrix. [*Plan Quality Management; Manage Quality*]

- **Matrix Based Charts** – Matrix-based chart showing connections between work packages and team members. Show all activities associated with each person and vice versa. [*Plan Resource Management*]

- **Mind Mapping** – Consolidating ideas created through individual brainstorming sessions into a single map to reflect commonalities and differences in understanding and to generate new ideas. [*Collect Requirements; Plan Quality Management; Plan Stakeholder Engagement*]
- **Probability and Impact Matrix** – Maps the probability of occurrence of each risk and its impact on project objectives if that risk occurs. [*Perform Qualitative Analysis*]
- **Scatter Diagrams** – Shows relationship between two variables. Identify possible relationships between independent and dependent variables. [*Manage Quality; Control Quality*]
- **Stakeholder Engagement Assessment Matrix** – Used to graphical show the comparison between current and desired stakeholder engagement levels. [*Plan Communications Management; Monitor Communications; Plan Stakeholder Engagement; Monitor Stakeholder Engagement*]
- **Stakeholder Mapping Representation** – Categorizing stakeholders using various methods (e.g., power/interest grid, stakeholder cube, salience model). [*Identify Stakeholders*]
- **Text Oriented Formats** – Position descriptions show team member responsibilities, authority, competencies, and qualifications outlined in a text document. [*Plan Resource Management*]

Decision Making Techniques

Select a course of action from different alternatives.

- **Multi-Criteria Decision Analysis** – Utilizing a decision matrix to provide a systematic analytical approach for establishing criteria, such as risk levels, uncertainty, and valuation, to evaluate and rank many ideas. [*Perform Integrated Change Control; Collect Requirements; Define Scope; Plan Quality Management; Manage Quality; Acquire Resources; Plan Risk Responses; Monitor Stakeholder Engagement*]
- **Voting** – Making decisions based on unanimity, majority, or plurality. [*Monitor and Control Project Work; Perform Integrated Change Control; Collect Requirements; Validate*

Notes

Scope; Estimate Activity Durations; Estimate Costs; Monitor Stakeholder Engagement]

Communication Skills

Transferring information between stakeholders.

- **Feedback** – Interactive communication between project manager and stakeholders (e.g., coaching, mentoring, and negotiating). [*Manage Communications; Monitor Stakeholder Engagement*]
- **Presentations** – Formal delivery of information and/ or documentation to project stakeholders (e.g., progress reports, background information to support decision making, general information about the project and its objectives). [*Manage Communications; Monitor Stakeholder Engagement*]

Interpersonal & Team Skills

Effectively lead and interact with team members and other stakeholders.

- **Active Listening** – Acknowledging, clarifying and confirming, understanding, and removing barriers that might cause miscommunication. [*Manage Project Knowledge; Manage Communications; Monitor Stakeholder Engagement*]
- **Communication Styles Assessment** – Identifying the preferred communication method, format, and content for stakeholders for planned communication activities. [*Plan Communication Management*]
- **Conflict Management** – Project manager will utilize the techniques to help bring stakeholders into alignment on the objectives, success criteria, requirements. [*Develop Project Charter; Develop Project Management Plan; Develop Team; Manage Team: Manage Communications; Manage Stakeholder Engagement*]
- **Culture Awareness** – Understanding the differences between individuals, groups, and organizations and adapting that throughout the project life cycle. [*Plan Communication*

Management; Manage Communications; Manage Stakeholder Engagement: Monitor Stakeholder Engagement]

- **Decision Making** – The ability to negotiate and influence the organization and the project management team. [*Manage Team*]

- **Emotional Intelligence** – Ability to identify, assesses, and manages the personal emotions of oneself and other people, as well as the collective emotions of groups of people. [*Manage Team*]

- **Facilitation** – Ability to effectively guide a group event to a successful decision, solution, or conclusion. [Develop Project Charter; Develop Project Management Plan; Manage Project Knowledge; Collect Requirements; Define Scope; Identify Risks; Perform Qualitative Risk Analysis; Perform Quantitative Risk Analysis; Plan Risk Responses]

- **Influencing** – Ability to compel people to behave or think in a certain way. Project Managers often don't have a lot of power of authority; they often need to use their influence. Project managers influence stakeholders by your knowledge, charisma, trust or reputation. [*Develop Team; Manage Team; Control Resources; Implement Risk Responses*]

- **Leadership** – Project managers to communicate the vision and inspire the project team to focus on the appropriate knowledge and knowledge objectives. [*Manage Project Knowledge; Manage Team; Monitor Stakeholder Engagement*]

- **Meeting Management** – Project managers to ensure the meetings that are being run are effective and efficient. [*Develop Project Charter; Develop Project Management Plan; Manage Communications*]

- **Motivation** – Project managers providing reasons for the team to act. Project teams are motivated by empowering them to participate in decision making and encouraging them to work independently. [*Develop Team*]

- **Negotiation** – Process that involves activities needed to resolve different kinds of disputes by conducting consultations between the involved parties to reach a consensus. Negotiations can happen at any time within the project management life cycle and it can be either formal or non-formal. [*Acquire Resources; Develop Team; Control Resources; Conduct Procurement; Manage Stakeholder Engagement*]

- **Networking** – Informal and formal social interaction and online social networking among project stakeholders which establishes and creates the conditions to share tacit and explicit knowledge. [*Manage Project Knowledge; Manage Communications; Monitor Stakeholder Engagement*]
- **Nominal Group Technique** – Ranks the ideas from a brain storming session in priority order. [*Collect Requirements*]
- **Observation/Conversation** – Providing a direct way of viewing individuals in their environment and how they perform their jobs or tasks and carry out processes. [*Collect Requirements; Monitor Communications; Manage Stakeholder Engagement*]
- **Political Awareness** – Helps the project manager to plan communications based on the project environment as well as the organization's political environment. [*Manage Project Knowledge; Plan Communications; Manage Communications; Manage Stakeholder Engagement; Monitor Stakeholder Engagement*]
- **Team Building** – Conducting activities that enhance the team's social relations and build a collaborative and cooperative working environment. [*Develop Team*]

Project Environments

Organizational Types

Functional – Organization grouped by areas of specialization within different functional areas. Team members work for a department half time and assigned to a project for half time. Team members return to their departments after project closure. The PM has little or no power. The power rests with the functional manager.

Projectized – Organization structured by projects. PM has the power. Team members are allocated 100 percent to the project. Once the project ends, they need to find another project.

Notes

Balanced Matrix – Functional Manger and Project Manager share power. Team members report to both. Communication is more complex.

Project Based Organization – Creates a temp framework around projects to achieve strategic goals

Weak Matrix – Power resides with the functional manager. Project Manager has very little power. PM acts as a Project Coordinator or Project Expeditor.

- **Project Coordinator** – Project coordinators have the power to make some decisions, have some authority, and report to a higher-level manager.
- **Project Expeditor** – A project expediter works as staff assistant and communications coordinator. The expediter cannot personally make or enforce decisions.

Project Management Office (PMO)

Organizational structure that standardizes the project related governance processes and facilities the sharing of resources, methodologies, tools, and techniques. There are three types of PMO:

Supportive – Provides a consultative role to the projects by supplying templates, best practices, training, etc. It serves as a respiratory of information; it will recommend but not require its templates be used. The control of this PMO is low.

Controlling – Provides support and requires compliance through various means. Requires certain templates to be used, adapting to the project framework or methodologies, and/ or conformance to governance framework. The control of this PMO is moderate.

Directive – Takes control of the projects by directing managing the projects. PMs are assigned and report directly to the PMO. The control of this PMO is high.

* Always assume a PMO unless specified otherwise in the question.

MASTERING THE PMP® EXAM [TOTAL PREP]

Role of the Project Manager

Project Manager – Person assigned by the performing organization to lead the team that is responsible for achieving the project objectives. The project manager's reporting relationships are based on the organizational structure and project governance.

Table 2. Sphere of Influence and a Project Managers Competencies

Sphere of Influence	Competencies	Performing Integration
Project	Talent Triangle	Process Level
Organization	Dealing with People	Cognitive Level
Industry	Qualities and Skills of a Leader	Context Level
Professional Disciplines	Politics, Power, and Getting Things Done	
Across Disciplines	Leadership Styles Personality	

MASTERING THE PMP® EXAM [TOTAL PREP]

Technical Skills

- Focus on the critical technical project management elements for each project they manage.
- Tailor both traditional and agile tools, techniques, and methods for each project.
- Make time to plan thoroughly and prioritize diligently.
- Manage project elements, including, but not limited to, schedule, cost, resources, and risks.

Strategic and Business Management Skills

- Explain to others the essential business aspects of a project.
- Work with the project sponsor, team, and subject matter experts to develop an appropriate project delivery strategy.
- Implement that strategy in a way that maximizes the business value of the project.

Leadership Skills

- Dealing with People
- Qualities and SKILLS of a Leader
- Politics, Power, and Getting Things done

Project Manager Power

- **Positional:** Formal, Authoritative, Legitimate (e.g., formal position granted in the organization or team)
- **Referent:** Respect or admiration others hold for the individual, credibility gained
- **Expert:** Skill, information possessed; experience, training, education, certification)
- **Reward-oriented:** Ability to give praise, monetary or other desired items)
- **Punitive or Coercive:** Ability to invoke discipline or negative consequences)

Notes

MASTERING THE PMP® EXAM [TOTAL PREP]

Project Manager's Leadership

- **Laissez-Faire:** Allowing the team to make their own decisions and establish their own goals, also referred to as taking a hands-off style.

- **Transactional:** Focus on goals, feedback, and accomplishment to determine rewards; management by exception.

- **Servant Leader:** Demonstrates commitment to serve and put other people first; focuses on other people's growth, learning, development, autonomy, and well-being; concentrates on relationships, community and collaboration; leadership is secondary and emerges after service.

- **Transformational:** Empowering followers through idealized attributes and behaviors, inspirational motivation, encouragement for innovation and creativity, and individual consideration.

- **Charismatic:** Able to inspire; is high-energy, enthusiastic, self-confident; holds strong convictions.

- **Interactional:** A combination of transactional, transformational, and charismatic.

Project Manager's Personalities

- **Authentic:** Accepts others for what and who they are, shows open concern.
- **Courteous:** Ability to apply appropriate behavior and etiquette.
- **Creative:** Ability to think abstractly, to see things differently, to innovate.
- **Cultural:** Measure of sensitivity to other cultures including values, norms, and beliefs.
- **Emotional:** Ability to perceive emotions and the information they present and to manage them; measure of interpersonal skills.
- **Intellectual:** Measure of human intelligence over multiple aptitudes.
- **Managerial:** Measure of management practice and potential
- **Political:** Measure of political intelligence and making things happen
- **Service-Oriented:** Evidence of willingness to serve other people
- **Social:** Ability to understand and manage people
- **Systemic:** Drive to understand and build systems.

Initiating Process Group

- Two (2) processes
- Perform project assessment based upon available information, lessons learned from previous projects, and meetings with relevant stakeholders in order to support the evaluation of the feasibility of new products or services within the given assumptions and/or constraints.
- Identify key deliverables based on the business requirements in order to manage customer expectations and direct the achievement of project goals.
- Perform stakeholder analysis using appropriate tools and techniques in order to align expectations and gain support for the project.
- Identify high level risks, assumptions, and constraints based on the current environment, organizational factors, historical data, and expert judgment, in order to propose an implementation strategy.
- Participate in the development of the project charter by compiling and analyzing gathered information in order to ensure project stakeholders agree on its elements.
- Obtain project charter approval from the sponsor, in order to formalize the authority assigned to the project manager and gain commitment and acceptance for the project.
- Conduct benefit analysis with relevant stakeholders to validate project alignment with organizational strategy and expected business value.
- Inform stakeholders of the approved project charter to ensure common understanding of the key deliverables, milestones, and their roles and responsibilities.
- Knowledge and Skills:
- Analytical skills
- Benefit analysis techniques
- Elements of a project charter
- Estimation tools and techniques
- Strategic management

Notes

MASTERING THE PMP® EXAM [TOTAL PREP]

Table 3. Initiating Process Group ITTO Matrix

Knowledge Area	Processes	Inputs	Tools and Techniques	Outputs
Integration Management	**Develop Project Charter** The process of developing a document that formally authorizes a project or a phase and documenting initial requirements that satisfy the stakeholder's needs and expectations.	1. Project Statement of Work 2. Business Documents 3. Business Case 4. Agreements 5. Enterprise Environmental Factors 6. Organizational Process Assets	1. Expert Judgment 2. Data Gathering [*Brainstorming, Focus Groups, Interviews*] 3. Interpersonal and Team Skills [*Conflict Management, Facilitation, Meeting Management*] 4. Meetings	1. Project Charter 2. Assumption Log
Stakeholder Management	**Identify Stakeholders** This is the process of identifying all people or organizations impacted by the project, and documenting relevant information regarding their interests, expectation, involvement, and influence on project success.	1. Project Charter 2. Business Documents 3. Project Management Plan [*Communications Management Plan, Stakeholder Engagement Plan*] 4. Project Documents [*Change Log, Issue Log, Requirements Documentation*] 5. Agreements 6. Enterprise environmental factors 7. Organizational process assets	1. Expert Judgment 2. Data Gathering [*Questionnaires and Surveys, Brainstorming*] 3. Data Analysis [*Stakeholder Analysis, Document Analysis*] 4. Data Representation [*Stakeholder Mapping/ Representation*] 5. Meetings	1. Stakeholder Register 2. Change Requests 3. Project Management Plan Updates 4. Project Document Updates

Key Terms:

Integration Management

Business Case – A document that provides the required info from a business standpoint to determine whether the project is worth the investment.

Agreements – A document or communication that defines the initial intentions of a project (e.g., contract, memorandum of understanding (MOU), letters of agreement, verbal agreements, email, etc.)

Project Charter – Names the PM and formally authorizes him/her to expend resources to achieve project objectives and needs. Includes high-level requirements, risks, summary budget, milestone schedules, assumptions, and constraints, etc. Output of Develop Project Charter.

Assumption Log – Project document used to record all assumptions and constraints throughout the project life cycle. Output of Develop Project Charter.

Stakeholder Management

Stakeholder Register – Project document output from Identify Stakeholders that include the identification, assessment, and classification of identified stakeholders.

Benefit Measurement Methods

(Bigger is better for the following)

- Present Value (PV) = (1+ 1)
- Net Present Value (NPV) = PV – Cost Internal Rate of Return (I R): No formula
- Benefit Cost Ratio (BCR) = Benefit Cost Ratio.
  A BCR > 1 means benefit is greater,
  < 1 means cost is greater,
  = 1 means a break-even project
- Economic Value Add (EVA) = After tax profit – (Capital expenditures × Cost of capital)
- Return on Investment (ROI) = (Benefit – Cost)/Cost
- Return on Invested Capital (ROIC) = Net income (after tax) from project I Total capital Invested in the project

(Smaller is better for the following)

- Payback Period: The number of time periods to recoup initial costs of a project
- Opportunity Cost: The value of a project that Is not done so that another project can be executed
- Depreciation: Straight line, accelerated – double declining, sum or years digits

Planning Process Group

Those processes required to establish the scope of the project, refine the objectives and define the course of action required to attain the objectives that the project was undertaken to achieve. Develop a project management plan to utilize for implementing, tracking, monitoring and closing the project.

Notes

- Review and assess detailed project requirements, constraints, and assumptions with stakeholders based on the project charter, lessons learned, and by using requirement gathering techniques to establish detailed project deliverables.
- Develop a scope management plan, based on the approved project scope and using scope management techniques, to define, maintain, and manage the scope of the project.
- Develop the cost management plan based on the project scope, schedule, resources, approved project charter and other information, using estimating techniques, to manage project costs.
- Develop the project schedule based on the approved project deliverables and milestones, scope, and resource management plans to manage timely completion of the project.
- Develop the human resource management plan by defining the roles and responsibilities of the project team members to create a project organizational structure and provide guidance regarding how resources will be assigned and managed.
- Develop the communications management plan based on the project organizational structure and stakeholder requirements, to define and manage the flow of project information.
- Develop the procurement management plan based on the project scope, budget, and schedule, to ensure that the required project resources will be available.
- Develop the quality management plan and define the quality standards for the project and its products, based on the project scope, risks, and requirements, to prevent the occurrence of defects and control the cost of quality.
- Develop the change management plan by defining how changes will be addressed and controlled to track and manage change.
- Plan for risk management by developing a risk management plan; identifying, analyzing, and prioritizing project risk; creating the risk register; and defining risk response strategies to manage uncertainty and opportunity throughout the project life cycle.

- Present the project management plan to the relevant stakeholders according to applicable policies and procedures to obtain approval to proceed with project execution.
- Conduct kick-off meeting, communicating the start of the project, key milestones, and other relevant information to inform and engage stakeholders and gain commitment.
- Develop the stakeholder management plan by analyzing needs, interests, and potential impact to effectively manage stakeholders' expectations and engage them in project decisions.
- Knowledge and Skills:
    - Change management planning
    - Cost management planning, including project budgeting tools and techniques
    - Communications planning
    - Contract types and selection criteria
    - Estimation tools and techniques
    - Human resource planning
    - Lean and efficiency principles
    - Procurement planning
    - Quality management planning
    - Requirements gathering techniques (e.g., planning sessions, brainstorming, and focus groups)
    - Regulatory and environmental impacts assessment planning
    - Risk management planning
    - Scope deconstruction (e.g., WBS, Scope backlog) tools and techniques
    - Scope management planning
    - Stakeholder management planning
    - Time management planning, including scheduling tools and techniques
    - Workflow diagramming techniques

MASTERING THE PMP® EXAM [TOTAL PREP]

Table 4. Planning Process Group ITTO Matrix

Knowledge Area	Process	Inputs	Tools and Techniques	Outputs
Integration Management.	**Develop Project Management Plan** The process of documenting the actions necessary to define, prepares, integrate, and coordinate all subsidiary plans.	1. Project Charter 2. Outputs from other processes 3. EEF's 4. OPA's	1. Expert Judgment 2. Data Gathering [Brainstorming, Checklists, Focus Groups, Interviews] 3. Interpersonal and team skills [Conflict Management, Facilitation, Meeting Management] 4. Meetings	1. Project Management Plan
Scope Management	**Plan Scope Management** The process of developing a scope management plan that defines how project scope will be defined, validated and controlled.	2. Project Management Plan 3. Project charter 4. EEF's 5. OPA's	6. Expert Judgment 7. Meetings	8. Scope Management Plan 9. Requirements Management Plan
Scope Management (continued)	**Collect Requirements** The process of defining and documenting stakeholders' needs to meet the project objectives.	1. Project Charter 2. Project Management Plan [Scope Management Plan, Requirements Management Plan, Stakeholder Engagement Plan] 3. Project Documents [Assumption Log, Lessons Learned Register, Stakeholder Register] 4. Business Documents 5. Agreements 6. EEF's 7. OPA's	1. Expert Judgment 2. Data Gathering [Brainstorming, Interviews, Focus Groups, Questionnaires and Surveys, Benchmarking] 3. Data Analysis [Document Analysis] 4. Decision Making [Voting. Autocratic, Multi-Criteria] 5. Data Representation [Affinity Diagrams, Mind Mapping] 6. Interpersonal & Team Skills [Nominal Group Technique, Observation/ Conversation, Facilitation, Context Diagram, Protypes]	1. Requirements Documentation 2. Requirements Traceability Matrix
	Define Scope The process of developing the project scope statement that details project and project scope of the project. Includes detailed description of the deliverables, the acceptance criteria, assumptions and requirements of the project.	1. Project Charter 2. Project Management Plan [Scope Management Plan] 3. Project Documents [Requirements Documentation] 4. EEF's 5. OPA's	1. Expert judgment 2. Data Analysis [Alternative Analysis] 3. Decision Making 4. Interpersonal and Team Skills [Facilitated Workshops] 5. Product analysis	6. Project Scope Statement 7. Project Documents Updates

43

Notes

MASTERING THE PMP® EXAM [TOTAL PREP]

Knowledge Area	Process	Inputs	Tools and Techniques	Outputs
	Create WBS The process of subdividing project deliverables and project work into smaller, more manageable components.	1. Project Management Plan [*Scope Management Plan*] 2. Project Documents [*Project Scope Statement, Requirements Documentation*] 3. EEF's 4. OPA's	1. Expert Judgment 2. Decomposition	1. Scope Baseline [*WBS, WBS Dictionary, Project Scope Statement*] 2. Project Document Updates
Schedule Management	**Plan Schedule Management** The process of defining how the project schedule will be planned, developed, managed, executed, and controlled.	1. Project Charter 2. Project Management Plan [*Scope Management Plan, Development Approach*] 3. EEF's 4. OPA's	1. Expert Judgment 2. Data Analysis [*Analytical Techniques, Alternative Analysis*] 3. Meetings	1. Schedule Management Plan
	Define Activities The process of breaking down work packages into activities for cost estimating, scheduling, monitoring and controlling the project work.	1. Project Management Plan [*Schedule Management Plan, Scope Baseline*] 2. EEF's 3. OPA's	1. Expert Judgment 2. Decomposition 3. Rolling wave planning 4. Meetings	1. Activity list 2. Activity attributes 3. Milestone list 4. Change Requests 5. Project Management Plan Updates
	Sequence Activities The process of putting the activities in a logical order to determine their dependencies to establish an efficient schedule.	1. Project Management Plan [*Schedule Management Plan, Scope Baseline*] 2. Project Management Documents [*Activity List, Activity Attributes, Milestone List, Assumption Log*] 3. EEF's 4. OPA's	1. Precedence Diagramming Method (PDM) 2. Dependency Determination 3. Leads and lags 4. Project Management Information System	1. Project Schedule Network Diagrams 2. Project Document Updates
	Estimate Activity Durations The process of estimating the activities to determine the time needed to perform each task	1. Project Management Plan [*Schedule Management Plan*] 2. Project Documents [*Activity attributes, Activity list, Assumption Log, Lessons Learned Register, Milestone List, Project Team Assignments, Resource Breakdown Structure, Resource Calendars, Resource Requirements, Risk Register*] 3. EEF's 4. OPA's	1. Expert Judgment 2. Analogous estimating 3. Parametric estimating 4. Three-Point estimating 5. Bottom-Up Estimating 6. Data Analysis [*Alternative Analysis, Reserve Analysis*] 7. Decision Making [*Voting*] 8. Meetings	1. Activity Duration Estimates 2. Basis of Estimates 3. Project Documents Updates

MASTERING THE PMP® EXAM [TOTAL PREP]

Knowledge Area	Process	Inputs	Tools and Techniques	Outputs
Schedule Management *(continued)*	**Develop Schedule** The process of putting together a schedule baseline with realistic planned dates to complete the project.	1. Project Management Plan [*Schedule Management Plan, Scope Baseline*] 2. Project Management Documents [*Activity list, Activity Attributes, Assumption Log, Basis of Estimates, Duration Estimates, Lesson Learned Register, Milestone List, Project Network Diagrams, Project Team Assignments, Resource Calendars, Risk Register, Resource Breakdown Structure*] 3. EEF's 4. OPA	1. Schedule Network Analysis 2. Critical Path Method 3. Resource Optimization Techniques 4. Data Analysis [*What-If Scenario Analysis, Stimulation*] 5. Leads and lags 6. Schedule Compression 7. Project Management Information Systems 8. Agile Release Planning	1. Schedule Baseline 2. Project Schedule 3. Schedule Data 4. Project Calendars 5. Change Requests 6. Project Management Plan Updates 7. Project Documents Updates
Cost Management	**Plan Cost Management** The process of putting together a plan to estimate, tracks, and monitor and control the project costs.	1. Project Project Management [*Schedule Management Plan, Risk Management Plan*] 2. Project Management Documents [*Activity List, Activity Attributes, Project Network Diagrams, Activity Resource Requirements, Resource Calendars, Activity Duration Estimates, Project Scope Statement, Risk Register, Project Staff Assignments, Resource Breakdown Structure*] 3. EEF's 4. OPA's	1. Expert judgment 2. Data Analysis [*Analytical techniques, Alternative Analysis*] 3. Meetings	1. Cost Management Plan

46

MASTERING THE PMP® EXAM [TOTAL PREP]

Knowledge Area	Process	Inputs	Tools and Techniques	Outputs
Cost Management *(continued)*	**Estimate Costs** The process of developing an approximation of the costs of each activity needed by identifying various approaches and their cost effectiveness.	1. Project Management Plan [*Cost Management Plan, Quality Management Plan, Quality Management Plan, Scope Baseline*] 2. Project Documents [*Lesson Learned Register, Project Schedule, Resource Requirements, Risk Register*] 3. EEF's 4. OPA's	1. Expert Judgment 2. Analogous Estimating 3. Parametric Estimating 4. Bottom-up estimating 5. Three-Point estimating 6. Data Analysis [*Alternative Analysis, Reserve Analysis, Cost of Quality*] 7. Project Management Information System 8. Decision Making [*Voting*]	1. Activity Cost Estimates 2. Basis of Estimates 3. Project Documents Updates
	Determine Budget The process of aggregating the estimated costs to establish an authorized time phased budget.	1. Project Management Plan [*Cost Management Plan, Resource Management Plan, Scope Baseline*] 2. Project Documents [*Basis of Estimates, Cost Estimates, Project Schedule, Risk Register*] 3. Agreements 4. EEF's 5. OPA's	1. Expert Judgment 2. Cost aggregation 3. Data Analysis [*Reserve Analysis*] 4. Historical relationships 5. Funding limit reconciliation 6. Financing	1. Cost Baseline 2. Project Funding Requirements 3. Project Documents Updates
Quality Management	**Plan Quality Management** The process of defining quality requirements for the project and its deliverables. Documenting a plan that a project team can utilize as guidance on how to manage and validate quality throughout the project.	1. Project Charter 2. Project Management Plan [*Requirements Management Plan, Risk Management Plan, Stakeholder Engagement Plan, Scope Baseline*] 3. Project Documents [*Assumption Log, Requirements Documentation, RTM, Risk Register, Stakeholder Register*] 4. EEF's 5. OPA's	1. Expert Judgment 2. Data Gathering [*Benchmarking, Brainstorming, Interviews*] 3. Data Analysis [*Cost-Benefit Analysis, Cost of Quality*] 4. Decision Making [*Multi Criteria*] 5. Data Representation [*Flowcharts, Logical Data Model, Matrix Diagrams, Mind Mapping*] 6. Test and Inspection Planning 7. Meetings	1. Quality Management Plan 2. Process Improvement Plan 3. Quality Metrics 4. Project Management Plan Updates 5. Project Documents Updates

Notes

MASTERING THE PMP® EXAM [TOTAL PREP]

Knowledge Area	Process	Inputs	Tools and Techniques	Outputs
Resource Management	**Plan Resource Management** The process of defining how to estimate, acquire, manage and use team and physical resources.	1. Project Charter 2. Project Management Plan [*Quality Management Plan, Scope Baseline*] 3. Project Documents [*Project Schedule, Requirements Documentation, Risk Register, Stakeholder Register*] 4. EEF's 5. OPA's	1. Expert Judgment 2. Data Representation [*Hierarchal Charts, Responsibility Assignment Matrix, Text Orientated Formats*] 3. Organizational theory 4. Meetings	1. Resource Management Plan 2. Team Charter 3. Project Documents Updates
	Estimate Activity Resources The process of estimating human resources required to perform each schedule activity.	1. Project Management Plan [*Resource Management Plan, Scope Baseline*] 2. Project Documents [*Activity List, Activity Attributes, Assumption Log, Cost Estimates, Resource Calendars, Risk Register*] 3. EEF's 4. OPA's	1. Expert Judgment 2. Bottom-up Estimating 3. Analogous Estimating 4. Parametric Estimating 5. Data Analysis [*Alternate Analysis*] 6. Project Management Information System 7. Meetings	1. Activity Resource Requirements 2. Resource Breakdown Structure 3. Project Documents Updates
Communications Management	**Plan Communications Management** The process of identifying the information and communication needs of the people involved in a project by determining what needs to be communicated, when, to whom, with what method, in which format and how frequently.	1. Project Management Plan [*Resource Management Plan, Stakeholder Engagement Plan*] 2. Project Documents [*Requirements Documentation, Stakeholder Register*] 3. EEF's 4. OPA's	1. Expert Judgment 2. Communication Requirements Analysis 3. Communication Technology 4. Communication Models 5. Communication Methods 6. Interpersonal and Team Skills [*Communication Styles Assessment, Political Awareness, Cultural Awareness*] 7. Data Representation [*Stakeholder Engagement Matrix*] 8. Meetings	1. Communications Management Plan 2. Project Management Plan Updates 3. Project Documents Updates
Risk Management	**Plan Risk Management** The process deciding how to approach, plan and execute positive and negative risks.	1. Project Management Plan 2. Project Charter 3. Project Documents [*Stakeholder Register*] 4. Enterprise Environmental Factors 5. Organizational Process Assets	1. Data Analysis [*Stakeholder Analysis*] 2. Expert Judgment 3. Meetings	1. Risk Management Plan

MASTERING THE PMP® EXAM [TOTAL PREP]

Knowledge Area	Process	Inputs	Tools and Techniques	Outputs
	Identify Risks The process of identifying all negative and positive risks on a project.	1. Project Management Plan [Risk Management Plan, Cost Management Plan, Schedule Management Plan, Quality Management Plan, Resource Management Plan, Scope Baseline] 2. Project Management Documents [Assumption Log, Activity Cost Estimates, Activity Duration Estimates, Stakeholder Register, Issue Log, Lessons Learned Register, Requirements Documentation, Resource Requirements] 3. Agreements 4. Procurement Documents 5. Enterprise Environmental Factors 6. Organizational Process Assets	1. Expert Judgment 2. Data Analysis [Documentation Analysis, Assumptions and Constraints Analysis, SWOT Analysis, Root Cause Analysis] 3. Data Gathering [Brainstorming, Checklists, Interviews] 4. Interpersonal and Team Skills [Facilitation] 5. Prompt Lists 6. Meetings	1. Risk Register 2. Risk Report 3. Project Document Updates
Risk Management (continued)	**Perform Qualitative Risk Analysis** The process of prioritizing the identified risks for subsequent further analysis or action by assessing and combining their probability of occurrence and impact	1. Project Management Plan [Risk Management Plan] 2. Project Documents [Assumption Log, Risk Register, Stakeholder Register] 3. Enterprise Environmental Factors 4. Organizational Process Assets	1. Expert Judgment 2. Data Gathering [Interviews] 3. Risk Analysis [Risk Data Quality Assessment, Risk Probability and Impact Assessment, Assessment of other Risk Parameters] 4. Interpersonal and Team Skills [Facilitation] 5. Risk Categorization 6. Data Representation [Probability and Impact Matrix, Hierarchical Charts] 7. Meetings	1. Risk Register Updates

MASTERING THE PMP® EXAM [TOTAL PREP]

Knowledge Area	Process	Inputs	Tools and Techniques	Outputs
	Perform Quantitative Risk Analysis The process of numerically analyzing the effect of overall project objectives of identified risks. This step might be skipped, depending on the project.	1. Project Management Plan [*Risk Management Plan, Cost Management Plan, Schedule Management Plan, Scope Baseline*] 2. Project Document [*Assumption Log, Basis of Estimates, Cost Estimates, Cost Forecasts, Duration Estimates, Milestone List, Resource Requirements, Risk Requirements, Risk Register, Risk Report, Schedule Forecasts*] 3. Enterprise Environmental Factors 4. Organizational Process Assets	1. Expert Judgment 2. Data Gathering [*Interviews*] 3. Interpersonal and Team Skills [*Facilitation*] 4. Representations of Uncertainty Data Representation Techniques 5. Data Analysis [*Simulation, Sensitivity Analysis, Decision Tree Analysis, Influence Diagrams*]	1. Risk Register Updates
Risk Management *(continued)*	**Plan Risk Responses** The process of developing options and actions to enhance opportunities and reduce threats to project objectives.	1. Project Management Plan [*Risk Management Plan, Resource Management Plan, Cost Baseline*] 2. Project Documents [*Lessons Learned Register, Project Schedule, Project Team Assignments, Resource Calendars, Risk Register, Risk Report, Stakeholder Register*] 3. EEF's 4. OPA's	1. Expert Judgment 2. Data Gathering [*Interviews*] 3. Interpersonal and Team Skills [*Facilitation*] 4. Strategies for Threats 5. Strategies for Opportunities 6. Contingent Response Strategies 7. Strategies for overall Project Risk 8. Data Analysis [*Alternative Analysis, Cost-Benefit Analysis*] 9. Decision Making [*Multicriteria Decision Analysis*]	1. Change Requests 2. Project Management Plan Updates 3. Project Documents Updates

Notes

Knowledge Area	Process	Inputs	Tools and Techniques	Outputs
Procurement Management	**Plan Procurement Management** The process of documenting project purchasing decisions, specifying the approach, and identifying potential sellers.	1. Project Charter 2. Business Documents 3. Project Management Plan [Scope Management Plan, Scope Management Plan, Quality Management Plan, Resource Management Plan, Scope Baseline] 4. Project Documents [Milestone List, Project Team Assignments, Requirements Documentation, RTM, Risk Register, Stakeholder Register] 5. EEF's 6. OPA's	1. Data Gathering [Market Research] 2. Data Analysis [Make or Buy Analysis] 3. Expert Judgment 4. Source Selection Criteria 5. Meetings	1. Procurement Management Plan 2. Procurement Strategy 3. Bid Documents 4. Procurement Statement of Work 5. Source Selection Criteria 6. Make or buy decisions 7. Independent Cost Estimates 8. Change Requests 9. Project Documents Updates 10. Organizational Process Assets Updates
acStakeholder Management	**Plan Stakeholder Engagement** The process of developing an approach to involve project stakeholders based on their needs, expectations, interests and potential impact on the project.	1. Project Charter 2. Project Management Plan [Resource Management Plan, Communications Management Plan, Risk Management Plan] 3. Project Documents [Assumption Log, Change Log, Issue Log, Project Schedule, Risk Register, Stakeholder Register] 4. Agreements 5. EEF's 6. OPA's	1. Expert Judgment 2. Data Gathering [Benchmarking] 3. Data Analysis [Assumption and Constraint Analysis, Root Cause Analysis] 4. Decision Making [Periodization/ Ranking] 5. Data Representation [Mind Mapping, Stakeholder Engagement Assessment Matrix] 6. Meetings	1. Stakeholder Engagement Plan

Integration Management

Project Management Plan: A single-approved document that defines how project is executed, monitored, controlled, and closed.

Scope Management

Work Breakdown Structure (WBS): A deliverable-oriented hierarchical decomposition or the work to be executed.

WBS Dictionary: Detailed description of the work to be done for each work package

WBS Creation Methods: By project phases, by major deliverables or subprojects, or by external subprojects.

Scope Baseline: A combination of approved project scope statement, WBS, WBS dictionary, and all approved changes.

Product Analysis: Techniques used for performing a detailed analysis to translate project objectives into tangible deliverables and requirements.

Requirements Traceability Matrix: A requirements mapping that links requirements to their origin and traces them throughout the project life cycle.

Scope Creep: Unapproved and undocumented changes.

Schedule Management

Schedule Network Analysis: Critical path method (CPM), critical chain method, what-if analysis, and resource leveling

Critical Path Method (CPM): A schedule analysis to calculate critical path, scheduling flexibility, and overall schedule

Critical Path: The longest path through a network diagram and determines the shortest time to complete the project; the path of highest risk if any of the activities on it gets delayed.

Activity-on-Node (AON) diagram: A basic type of a logic diagram used in scheduling

Critical Activity: Any activity in the schedule that does not possess any float; Total Float=0

Critical Path: The longest path through a network diagram and determines the shortest time to complete the project; if any activities are the path get delayed then the project will be delayed

Critical Path Method (CPM): Any calculation method that shows the Critical Path in the schedule

Duration: The amount of time required to complete a schedule activity

Early Start (ES): Earliest date the activity can start

Early Finish (EF): Earliest date that the activity can finish

Free Float (FF): The maximum number of days the activity can be delayed without delaying any succeeding activity

Lag: Planned wait time between activities

Lead: A lead may be used to indicate that an activity can start before its predecessor activity is completed. For example, editing of a book may start before the write-up is finished.

Late Finish (LF): Latest date that the activity can finish without causing a delay to the project completion date.

Late Start (LS): Latest date that the activity can start without causing a delay to the project completion date.

Predecessor: The "before" activity; immediately precedes

Successor: The "after" activity; immediately follows

Total Float (TF): The maximum number of days the activity can be delayed without delaying the project completion date.

Analogous Estimating: It is a top down, expert Judgment based on previous similar historical projects. It is less accurate because no two projects are identical. It is less costly and time consuming. Used in cases where there are only limited amounts of available information early in the project.

Parametric Estimating: Uses mathematical models based on historical records from other projects. Used only when a statistical relationship between historical data and current work can be established;

Three Points/PERT: Takes optimistic, pessimistic, and most likely estimates and provides a risk-based expected duration estimate by taking a weighted average.

Notes

Fast Tracking: Doing critical path activities in parallel when originally planned in series. More potential for conflicts, risks and rework.

Crashing: Adding additional resources to an activity. This is done when the project has additional funds for resources. This adds cost and mgmt. time.

Bar/Gantt: A time-phased graphical display of activity start dates, end dates, and durations; useful for tracking progress and reporting to team

Network Diagram: A schematic display of the sequential and logical relationships of the activities

Milestone Chart: Like a bar chart but only shows major events. A good tool for reporting to management and customers.

Activity Attributes: Detailed info about activities (e.g., duration, location)

Rolling Wave Planning: Planning work in near term in detail and future work at a higher level

Resource Breakdown Structure: A graphical and hierarchical structure of the identified resources arranged by resource category and type

Precedence Diagramming Method (PDM): A method to create a schematic display of the sequential and logical relationships of activities

Network Diagram: A schematic display of the sequential and logical relationships of the activities. Also called Activity-on-node (AON)

Resource Histogram: A graphical display of number of resources used in project throughout the project life cycle

Finish-to-Start (FS): A logical relationship in which a successor activity cannot start until a predecessor activity has finished. (Development cannot be started until the design is finished)

Finish-to-Finish (FF): A logical relationship in which a successor activity cannot finish until a predecessor activity has finished. (The broadcast of a football match cannot finish until the match is finished. So, the match is not depended on broadcast, but the broadcast is, if the match takes longer than the initial estimated time broadcast will also continue till that time.)

Start-to-Start (SS): A logical relationship in which a successor activity cannot start until a predecessor activity has started. (The activity of marketing brochure preparation cannot start until user documentation has started)

Start-to-Finish (SF): A logical relationship in which a successor activity cannot finish until a predecessor activity has started. (The first security guard shift (successor) cannot finish until the second security guard shift (predecessor) starts)

Mandatory: Unavoidable dependencies, hard logic, not in PM's control. Something the team must adhere too (e.g., must designing before building)

Discretionary: Preferred or soft dependencies, soft logic or preferred logic

External Dependency: Needing third party approval (needing a Government permit to proceed)

Schedule Baseline: Approved version of the project schedule that can be changed only through formal change control procedures and is used as a basis for comparison to actual results. It is also used as a reference to compare with the actual results to determine if a change, corrective action, or preventive action is necessary.

Cost Management

Life Cycle Costing: Taking into consideration the whole life of the product, and not just the cost of the project. (e.g., how much it will cost to maintain it.)

Value Engineering: Finding a less costly way to do the same way without impacting the scope and quality.

Working Capital: Current Assets – Current Liabilities

Cost Aggregation: Rolling up activity cost estimates to work packages; these estimates are then aggregated for the higher component levels of the WBS and then for the entire project.

Contingency Reserves: Money added to the project cost estimates by the project manager for uncertain events/risks that might happen (also known as "known unknowns"). This is included in the cost baseline.

Management Reserves: Money added to the project overall budget by the senior management for uncertain events that are not even thought of (also known as "unknown unknowns", i.e. risks not shown in the risk register). This is included in the cost budget not baseline.

Funding limit Reconciliation: Comparing the planned expenditure of project funds against any limits on the commitment of funds for the project to identify any variances between the funding limits and the planned expenditures.

Cost Baseline: The approved time-phased spending plan for the project on which the project cost performance is to be measured against. Changes to the Cost Baseline must undergo proper change management processes.

Cost Budget: Estimate of total amount of money required for carrying out the Project, including money set aside for identified and unidentified risks (i.e. unknown unknowns)

Cost Types:

Variable Costs: Costs that change with the amount of work involved with a project. (e.g., hourly rate, supplies, materials).

Fixed Costs: Costs that don't change throughout the life cycle of the project. (e.g., rent, setup costs, rental costs).

Notes

Direct Costs: Expenses directly associated with the project. (e.g., team wages, rewards, training, travel).

Indirect Costs: Costs that are shared and allocated among several or all projects. (e.g., fringe benefits)

Sunk Costs: Costs that have been spent and won't be recoverable. Project had ended and now restarting from start.

Opportunity Cost: Value of the project not chosen. (e.g., project A cost $20,000 and project B cost $30,000. You pick project A; the opportunity cost is project B.)

Quality Management:

Quality Metrics: Describe a project or product attribute to define how quality will be measured

Marginal Analysis: Looking for the point where benefits from improving quality equal the incremental cost to achieve that quality

Just in Time (JIT): Bringing inventory down to zero or almost near to a zero level

Benchmarking: Comparing actual or planned practices to those of other projects either inside the organization or outside to determine any improvements.

Design of Experiments (DOE): A what-If analysis of alternatives to identify which factors might improve quality.

Statistical Sampling: Choosing part of a population of interest for inspection instead of measuring the entire population

Quality Checklist: A component-specific, structured tool to verify all required steps have been performed.

Mutual Exclusivity: Two events are mutually exclusive if they cannot both occur in a single trial. (e.g., can't get a head and tail at the same time)

Statistical Independence: Likelihood of one event occurring does not affect the likelihood of another event occurring. (e.g., getting a 6 on a dice doesn't affect getting a 6 the next time around)

Prevention over Inspection: Quality should be planned, designed, and built in, not inspected in. It will cost more, and product will be poor quality.

Process Analysis: A part of the continuous improvement effort to look at process improvement from an organizational and technical point of view to determine where how to better improve the process.

Attribute Sampling: A method of measuring quality that consists of noting the presence or absence of some characteristic (attribute) in each of the units under consideration.

Total Quality Management (TQM): Technique or strategy that is implemented to assure that an awareness of quality is embedded in all phases of the project from conception to completion. Everyone is responsible for quality.

Continuous Improvement: Always looking to improve policies and process.

Resource Management:

Team Charter: Document developed part of the resource management plan that defines the purpose of the team, how they will work, and expected outcomes for the project.

Tuckman Ladder: The five stages of team building. Forming, Storming, Norming, Performing and Adjourning.

Procurement Management:

Statement of Work (SOW): Describe the work and activities that the seller is required to complete. The activities also include meetings, reports and communications.

Make or Buy Analysis: Determining whether a product can be cost effective if produced in house or outsourced.

Procurement Documents: Documents that are used to solicit proposals from perspective sellers. (e.g., RFP, RFQ, RFI)

Screening System: A set of minimum criteria set by the organization for the seller to meet in order to be considered for contract award.

Letter of Intent: Providing a letter to the buyer expressing the intention of hiring him/her.

Risk Management:

Risk Categories: A group of potential causes for risk (e.g., technical, political, external, project, environmental, etc.)

Risk Breakdown Structure (RBS): A comprehensive way of ordering risks according to their source.

Risk Triggers: Symptoms or warning signs that a potential risk is about to occur.

Risk Appetites: Acceptable level of risk in the project.

Risk Tolerances: Areas where risks can be acceptable or unacceptable.

Risk Threshold: Amount of risk that is acceptable

Residual Risks: Risks that remain after execution of risk response planning

Contingency Plan: Specific action that will be taken if opportunities or threats occur

Secondary Risk: A new risk created due to the implementation of the selected risk response strategy

Fallback Plan: Specific action that will be taken if contingency plan is not effective

Workarounds: Unplanned responses developed to deal with unanticipated risk events

Watch List: A list of low-priority, non-critical risks

Notes

Risk Tools:

SWOT Analysis: Strengths, weaknesses, opportunities, and threats analysis

Expected Monetary Value (EMV): Probability × Impact

Decision Tree: Used to make decision regarding Individual risk using EMV

Sensitivity Analysis (aka Tornado Diagram): Helps to determine which risks have the most potential impact on a project by examining all the uncertain elements at their baseline values.

MASTERING THE PMP® EXAM [TOTAL PREP]

Executing Process Group

Those processes performed to complete the work defined in the project management plan to satisfy the project requirements.

- Acquire and manage project resources by following the human resource a procurement management plans in order to meet project requirements.
- Manage task execution based on the project management plan by leading and developing the project team in order to achieve project deliverables.
- Implement the quality management plan using the appropriate tools and techniques in order to ensure that work is performed in accordance with required quality standards.
- Implement approved changes and corrective actions by following the change management plan in order to meet project requirements.
- Implement approved actions by following the risk management plan in order to minimize the impact of the risks and take advantage of opportunities on the project.
- Manage the flow of information by following the communications plan in order to keep stakeholders engaged and informed.
- Maintain stakeholder relationships by following the stakeholder management plan in order to receive continued support and manage expectations.
- Knowledge and Skills:
- Continuous improvement processes
- Contract management techniques
- Elements of a statement of work
- Interdependencies among project elements
- Project budgeting tools and techniques
- Quality standard tools
- Vendor management techniques

MASTERING THE PMP® EXAM [TOTAL PREP]

Table 5. Executing Process Group ITTO Matrix

Knowledge Area	Process	Inputs	Tools and Techniques	Outputs
Integration Management.	**Direct and Manage Project Work** The process of performing the work defined in the project management plan to complete the project deliverables.	1. Project Management Plan [*Any Component*] 2. Project Documents [*Change Log, Lessons Learned Register, Milestone List, Project Communications, Project Schedule, RTM, Risk Report, Risk Report*] 3. Approved Change Requests 4. Enterprise Environmental Factors 5. Organizational Process Assets	1. Expert Judgment 2. Project Management Information System 3. Meetings	1. Deliverables 2. Work Performance Data 3. Issue log 4. Change Requests 5. Project Management Plan Updates [*Any Component*] 6. Project Document Updates [*Activity list, Assumption log, Lessons Learned Register, Requirements Documentation, Risk Register, Stakeholder Register*] 7. Organizational Process Assets
	Manage Project Knowledge The process of using existing knowledge and creating new knowledge to achieve the project objectives and contribute to organizational learning.	1. Project Management Plan [All component] 2. Project Documents [*Lessons Learned Register, Project Team Assignments, Resource Breakdown Structure, Stakeholder Register*] 3. Approved Change Requests 4. Enterprise Environmental Factors 5. Organizational Process Assets	1. Expert Judgment 2. Knowledge Management 3. Information Management 4. Interpersonal and Team Skills [*Active Listening, Facilitation, Leadership, Networking, Political awareness*]	1. Lessons Learned Register 2. Project Management Plan Updates [*Any component*] 3. Organizational Process Assets Updates

Notes

MASTERING THE PMP® EXAM [TOTAL PREP]

Knowledge Area	Process	Inputs	Tools and Techniques	Outputs
Quality Management	**Manage Quality** The process of auditing the quality of deliverables to ensure the quality management plan is being adhered too and to continuously improve the process.	1. Project Management Plan [*Quality Management Plan*] 2. Project Management Documents [*Lessons Learned Register, Quality Control Measurements, Quality Metrics, Risk Report*] 3. Organization Process Assets	1. Data Gathering [*Checklists*] 2. Data Analysis [*Alternate Analysis, Document Analysis, Process Analysis, Root Cause Analysis*] 3. Decision Making [*Multi Criteria*] 4. Data Representation [*Affinity Diagrams, Cause and Effect Diagrams, Flowcharts, Histograms, Matrix Diagrams, Scatter Diagrams*] 5. Quality Audits 6. Design for X 7. Problem Solving 8. Quality Improvement Methods	1. Quality Reports 2. Test and Evaluations Documents 3. Change Requests 4. Project Management Plan Updates 5. Project Documents Updates
Resource Management	**Acquire Resources** The process of obtaining the best possible resources to build the project team for a successful completion of the project.	1. Project Management Plan [*Resource Management Plan, Procurement Management Plan, Cost Baseline*] 2. Project Documents [*Project Schedule, Resource Calendars, Resource Requirements, Stakeholder Register*] 3. Enterprise Environmental Factors 4. Organizational Process Assets	1. Interpersonal and Team Skills [*Negotiation*] 2. Pre-Assignment 3. Virtual Teams 4. Decision Making [*Multi-Criteria*]	1. Physical Resource Assignments 2. Project Team Assignments 3. Recourse calendars 4. Change Requests 5. Project Management Plan Updates 6. Project Documents Updates 7. Enterprise Environmental Updates 8. Organizational Process Updates

MASTERING THE PMP® EXAM [TOTAL PREP]

Knowledge Area	Process	Inputs	Tools and Techniques	Outputs
Resource Management (continued)	**Develop Team** The process of developing the project team to ensure decreased turnover, improved individual skills and improved team work.	1. Project Management Plan [*Resource Management Plan*] 2. Project Management Documents [*Lesson Learned Register, Project Schedule, Project Team Assignments, Resource Calendars, Team Charter*] 3. Enterprise Environmental Factors 4. Organizational Process Assets	1. Colocation 2. Virtual Team 3. Communication Technology 4. Interpersonal and Team Skills [*Conflict Management, Influencing, Motivation, Negotiation, Team Building*] 5. Recognition and Rewards 6. Training 7. Individual and Team Assessments 8. Meetings	1. Team Performance Assessments 2. Change Requests 3. Project Management Plan Updates 4. Project Documents Updates 5. Enterprise Environmental Factors Updates 6. Organizational Process Updates
	Manage Team The process of managing the team through observing, using issue logs, keeping in touch, completing performance appraisal, and resolving conflicts.	1. Project Management Plan [*Resource Management Plan*] 2. Project Management Documents [*Issue Log, Lessons Learned Register, Project Team Assignments, Team Charter*] 3. Work Performance Reports 4. Team Performance Assessments 5. Enterprise Environmental Factors 6. Organizational Process Assets	1. Interpersonal and Team Skills [*Conflict Management, Decision Making, Emotional Intelligence, Influencing, Leadership*] 2. Project Management Information System	1. Change Requests 2. Project Management Plan Updates 3. Project Documents Updates 4. Enterprise Environmental Factors Updates 5. Organizational Process Assets Updates

MASTERING THE PMP® EXAM [TOTAL PREP]

Knowledge Area	Process	Inputs	Tools and Techniques	Outputs
Communications Management	**Manage Communications** The process of ensuring timely and appropriate collection, creation, distribution, storage, retrieval, management, monitoring, and the ultimate disposition of project information as defined in the communications management plan.	1. Project Management Plan [*Resource Management Plan, Communications Management Plan, Stakeholder Engagement Plan*] 2. Project Documents [*Change Log, Issue Log, Lessons Learned Register, Quality Report, Risk Report, Stakeholder Register*] 3. Work Performance Reports 4. Enterprise Environmental Factors 5. Organizational Process Assets	1. Communication Technology 2. Communication Methods 3. Communication Skills [Communication Competence, Feedback, Nonverbal, Presentations] 4. Project Management Information Systems 5. Performance reporting 6. Interpersonal and Team Skills [*Active Listening, Conflict Management, Cultural Awareness, Meeting Management, Networking, Political Awareness*] 7. Meetings	1. Project Communications 2. Project Management Plan Updates 3. Project Documents Updates 4. Organizational Process Assets Updates
Risk Management	**Implement Risk Responses** The process of ensuring the risk owners are implementing agreed upon risk responses.	1. Project Management Plan [Risk Management Plan] 2. Project Documents [Lessons Learned Register, Risk Register, Risk Report] 3. Organizational Process Assets	1. Expert Judgment 2. Interpersonal and Team Skills [Influencing] 3. Project Management Information System	1. Change Requests 2. Project Documents Updates

Notes

MASTERING THE PMP® EXAM [TOTAL PREP]

Knowledge Area	Process	Inputs	Tools and Techniques	Outputs
Procurement Management	**Conduct Procurements** The process of obtaining seller responses, selecting a seller, and awarding a contract.	1. Project Management Plan [*Scope Management Plan, Requirements Management Plan, Communications Management Plan, Risk Management Plan, Procurement Management Plan, Configuration Management Plan, Cost Baseline*] 2. Project Documents [*Lessons Learned Register, Project Schedule, Requirements Documentation, Risk Register, Stakeholder Register*] 3. Procurement Documentation 4. Seller Proposals 5. Enterprise Environmental Factors 6. Organization Process Assets	1. Expert Judgment 2. Advertising 3. Bidder Conference 4. Data Analysis [*Proposal Evaluation*] 5. Interpersonal and Team Skills [*Negotiations*]	1. Selected Sellers 2. Agreements 3. Change Requests 4. Project Management Plan Updates 5. Project Document Updates 6. Organizational Process Assets Updates
Stakeholder Management	**Manage Stakeholder Engagement** The process of communicating and working with stakeholders to meet their needs, address issues as they occur, and foster stakeholder engagement in project activities throughout the project life cycle.	1. Project Management Plan [*Communication Management Plan, Risk Management Plan, Stakeholder Engagement Plan, Change Management Plan*] 2. Project Documents [*Change Log, Issue Log, Lessons Learned Register, Stakeholder Register*] 3. Enterprise Environmental Factors 4. Organizational Process Assets	1. Expert Judgment 2. Communication Skills [*Feedback*] 3. Interpersonal and Team Skills [*Conflict Management, Cultural Awareness, Negotiation, Observation/ Conversation, Political Awareness*] 4. Ground rules 5. Meetings	1. Change Requests 2. Project Management Plan Updates 3. Project Document Updates

Integration Management

Work Performance Data: Current status of various project parameters (e.g., cost, schedule, quality, etc.) gathered while the team is performing their work to complete the project deliverables.

Resource Management

Virtual Team: Consists of a group of people who never or rarely meet but who have a shared goal of successful completion of the project.

Co-location: Placing project team members in the same physical location to enhance their ability to perform as a team.

Pre-Assignment: Identifying and assigning resources to be used in future projects.

Procurement Management

Bidder Conference: Meeting between the buyer and sellers before the submission of proposals or bids. Objective of the meeting is to ensure the sellers have a common understanding of the procurement requirements and that no potential sellers get special treatment from the buyer.

Source Selection Criteria: Set of attributes desired by the buyer which a seller is required to meet or exceed to be selected for a contract.

Monitoring and Controlling Process Group

The process which oversee all the tasks and metrics necessary to ensure that the approved and authorized project is within scope, on time, and on budget so that the project precedes with minimal risk. This process involves comparing actual performance with planned performance and taking corrective action to yield the desired outcome when significant differences exist. Monitoring and Controlling is continuously performed throughout the life of the project.

- Measure project performance using appropriate tools and techniques in order to identify and quantify any variances and corrective actions.
- Manage changes to the project by following the change management plan in order to ensure that project goals remain aligned with business needs.
- Verify that project deliverables conform to the quality standards established in the quality management plan by using appropriate tools and techniques to meet project requirements and business needs.
- Monitor and assess risk by determining whether exposure has changed and evaluating the effectiveness of response strategies in order to manage the impact of risks and opportunities on the project.
- Review the issue log, update if necessary, and determine corrective actions by using appropriate tools and techniques in order to minimize the impact on the project.
- Capture, analyze, and manage lessons learned, using lessons learned management techniques in order to enable continuous improvement.
- Monitor procurement activities according to the procurement plan in order to verify compliance with project objectives.
- Knowledge and Skills:
- Performance measurement and tracking techniques (e.g., EV, CPM, PERT, Trend Analysis)
- Process analysis techniques (e.g., LEAN, Kanban, Six Sigma)
- Project control limits (e.g., thresholds, tolerance)
- Project finance principles
- Project monitoring tools and techniques
- Project quality best practices and standards (e.g., ISO, BS, CMMI, IEEE)
- Quality measurement tools (e.g., statistical sampling, control charts, flowcharting, inspection, assessment)
- Risk identification and analysis techniques
- Risk response techniques
- Quality validation and verification techniques

Notes

MASTERING THE PMP® EXAM [TOTAL PREP]

Table 6. Monitoring and Controlling Process Group ITTO Matrix

Knowledge Area	Process	Inputs	Tools and Techniques	Outputs
Integration Management	**Monitor and Control Project Work** The process of tracking, reviewing, and regulating the progress to meet the performance objectives defined in the project management plan.	1. Project Management Plan [*Any component*] 2. Project Documents [*Assumption log, Basis of Estimates, Cost Forecasts, Issue Log, Lessons Learned Register, Milestone List, Quality Reports, Risk Register, Risk Report, Schedule Forecasts*] 3. Work Performance Information 4. Agreements 5. Enterprise Environmental Factors 6. Organizational Process Assets	1. Expert Judgement 2. Data Analysis [*Alternatives Analysis, Cost-Benefit Analysis, Earned Value Analysis, Root Cause Analysis, Trend Analysis, Variance Analysis*] 3. Decision Making [*Voting*] 4. Meetings	1. Work Performance Information 2. Change Requests 3. Project Management Plan Updates [*Any component*] 4. Project Document Updates [*Cost Forecasts, Issue Log, Lessons Learned Register, Risk Register, Schedule Forecasts*]
	Performed Integrated Change Control The process of reviewing all change requests; approving changes and managing changes to deliverables, organizational process assets, and the project management plan; and communicating their disposition. Changes may be requested by any stakeholder involved with the project.	1. Project Management Plan [*Change Management Plan, Scope Baseline, Schedule Baseline, Cost Baseline*] 2. Project Documents [*Basis of Estimates, RTM, Risk Report*] 3. Work Performance Reports 4. Change Requests 5. Enterprise Environmental Factors 6. Organizational Process Assets	1. Expert Judgement 2. Change Control Tools 3. Data Analysis [*Alternate Analysis, Cost-Benefit Analysis*] 4. Decision Making [*Voting, Autocratic Decision Making, Multi-criteria Decision Analysis*] 5. Meetings	1. Approved Change Requests 2. Project Management Plan Updates [*Any component*] 3. Project Document Updates [*Change Log*]

77

MASTERING THE PMP® EXAM [TOTAL PREP]

Knowledge Area	Process	Inputs	Tools and Techniques	Outputs
Scope Management	**Validate Scope** The process of formalizing acceptance of the completed project deliverables. It brings objectivity to the acceptance process and increases the probability of final product, service, or result acceptance by validating each deliverable. This process is performed periodically throughout the project as needed.	1. Project Management Plan 2. Project Documents [*Requirements documentation, Requirements Traceability Matrix*] 3. Verified Deliverables 4. Work performance data	1. Project Management Plan 2. Project Documents [*Requirements documentation, Requirements Traceability Matrix*] 3. Verified Deliverables 4. Work performance data	1. Accepted Deliverables 2. Change Requests 3. Work Performance Information 4. Project Documents Updates
	Control Scope The process of monitoring the status of the project and product scope and managing changes to the scope baseline.	1. Project Management Plan 2. Project Documents [*Requirements Documentation, RTM*] 3. Work Performance Data 4. Organizational Process Assets	1. Data Analysis [*Variance Analysis*]	1. Work Performance Information 2. Change Requests 3. Project Management Plan Updates 4. Project Documents Updates
Schedule Management	Control Schedule Measure performance; determine variance, corrective and preventive actions.	1. Project Management Plan [*Schedule Management Plan, Schedule Baseline, Scope Baseline, Performance Measurement Baseline*] 2. Project Documents [*Lesson Learned Register, Project Calendars, Project Schedule, Resource Calendars, Schedule Data*] 3. Work Performance Data 4. Organizational Process Assets	1. Data Analysis [*Earned Value Analysis. Iteration Burndown Chart, Performance Reviews, Trend Analysis, Variance Analysis, What-if Scenario Analysis*] 2. Critical Path Method 3. Project Management Information System 4. Resource Optimization Techniques 5. Leads and lags 6. Schedule Compression	1. Work Performance Information 2. Schedule Forecasts 3. Change Requests 4. Project Management Plan Updates 5. Project Documents Updates

MASTERING THE PMP® EXAM [TOTAL PREP]

Knowledge Area	Process	Inputs	Tools and Techniques	Outputs
Cost Management	**Control Costs** The process for ensuring that costs are carefully monitored and controlled. It ensures that costs stay on track and those changes is detected whenever it occurs.	1. Project Management Plan [*Cost Management Plan, Cost Baseline, Performance Measure Baseline*] 2. Project Documents [*Lesson Learned Register*] 3. Project Funding Requirements 4. Work Performance Data 5. Organizational process assets	1. Expert Judgment 2. Data Analysis [*Earned Value Analysis, Variance Analysis, Trend Analysis, Reserve Analysis*] 3. To-Complete Performance Index (TCPI) 4. Project Management Information System	1. Work Performance Information 2. Cost Forecasts 3. Change Requests 4. Project Management Plan Updates 5. Project Documents Updates 6. Organizational Process Assets Updates
Quality Management	**Control Quality** The process of monitoring and recording results of executing the quality management activities in order to assess performance and ensure the project outputs are complete, correct, and meet customer expectations.	1. Project Management Plan [*Quality Management Plan*] 2. Project Documents [*Lessons Learned Register, Quality Metrics, Test and Evaluation Documents*] 3. Approved Change Requests 4. Deliverables 5. Enterprise Environmental Factors 6. Organizational Process Assets	1. Data Gathering [*Checklists, Check sheets, Statistical Sampling, Questionnaires and Surveys*] 2. Data Analysis [*Performance Reviews, Root Cause Analysis*] 3. Inspection 4. Testing/product evaluations 5. Data Representation [*Cause and Effect Diagrams, Control Charts, Histograms, Scatter Diagrams*] 6. Meetings	1. Quality control measurements 2. Verified Deliverables 3. Work Performance Information 4. Change requests 5. Project Management Plan Updates 6. Project Documents Updates
Resource Management	**Control Resources** The process of ensuring that the physical resources assigned and allocated to the projects are available as planned, as well as monitoring the planned versus the actual utilization of resources and taking corrective actions as necessary.	1. Project Management Plan [*Resource Management Plan*] 2. Project Documents [*Issue Log, Lessons learned register, Physical Resource Assignments, Project Schedule, Resource Breakdown Structure, Resource Requirements, Risk Register*] 3. Work Performance Data 4. Agreements 5. Organizational Process Assets	1. Data Analysis [*Alternatives Analysis, Cost-benefit Analysis, Performance Reviews, Trend Analysis*] 2. Problem Solving 3. Interpersonal and team skills [*Negotiation, Influencing*] 4. Project Management Information System	1. Work Performance Information 2. Change requests 3. Project Management plan Updates 4. Project Documents Updates

Notes

MASTERING THE PMP® EXAM [TOTAL PREP]

Knowledge Area	Process	Inputs	Tools and Techniques	Outputs
Communications Management	**Monitor Communications** The process of ensuring that the information needs of the project stakeholders is met by monitoring and controlling communication throughout the project life cycle.	1. Project Management Plan [*Resource Management Plan, Communications Management Plan, Stakeholder Engagement Plan*] 2. Project Documents [*Issue Log, Lessons Learned Register, Project Communications*] 3. Work Performance Data 4. Enterprise Environmental Factors 5. Organizational Process Assets	1. Expert Judgement 2. Project Management Information System 3. Data analysis [*Stakeholder Engagement Assessment Matrix*] 4. Interpersonal and team skills [*Observation/ Conversation, Communication Skills*] 5. Meetings	1. Work Performance Information 2. Change Requests 3. Project Management Plan Updates 4. Project Documents Updates
Risk Management	**Monitor Risks** The process of monitoring the implementation of agreed upon risk response plans, tracking identified risks, identifying and analyzing new risks, and evaluating risk process effectiveness throughout the project.	1. Project Management Plan [*Risk Management Plan*] 2. Project documents [*Issue Log, Lessons Learned Register, Risk Register Risk Report*] 3. Work Performance Data 4. Work Performance Reports	1. Data analysis [*Technical Performance Analysis, Reserve Analysis*] 2. Audits 3. Meetings	1. Work Performance Information 2. Change Requests 3. Project Management Plan Updates 4. Project Documents Updates
Procurement Management	**Control Procurement** The process of managing procurement relationships, monitoring contract performance, and making changes and corrections as needed.	1. Project Management Plan [*Resource Management Plan*] 2. Project Documents [*Issue Log, Lessons learned register, Physical Resource Assignments, Project Schedule, Resource Breakdown Structure, Resource Requirements, Risk Register*] 3. Work Performance Data 4. Agreements 5. Organizational Process Assets	1. Expert Judgment 2. Claims Administration 3. Data Analysis [*Performance Reviews, Earned Value Analysis, Trend Analysis*] 4. Inspection 5. Audits	1. Closed Procurements 2. Work Performance Information 3. Procurement Documentation Updates 4. Change Requests 5. Project Management Plan Updates 6. Project Documents Updates 7. Organizational Process Assets Updates

MASTERING THE PMP® EXAM [TOTAL PREP]

Knowledge Area	Process	Inputs	Tools and Techniques	Outputs
Stakeholder Management	**Monitor Stakeholder Engagement** The process of monitoring project stakeholder relationships and tailoring strategies for engaging stakeholders through modification of engagement strategies and plans	1. Project Management Plan [*Resource Management Plan, Communications Management Plan, Stakeholder Engagement Plan*] 2. Project Documents [*Issue Log, Lessons Learned Register, Project Communications, Risk Register, Stakeholder Register*] 3. Work Performance Data 4. Enterprise Environmental Factors 5. Organizational Process Assets	1. Data Analysis [*Alternatives Analysis, Root Cause Analysis, Stakeholder Analysis*] 2. Decision Making [*Multi-Criteria Decision Analysis, Voting*] 3. Data Representation [*Stakeholder Engagement Assessment Matrix*] 4. Communication skills [*Feedback, Presentations*] 5. Interpersonal and Team Skills [*Active Listening, Cultural Awareness, Leadership, Networking, Political Awareness*] 6. Meetings	1. Work Performance Information 2. Change Requests 3. Project Management Plan Updates 4. Project Documents Updates

Integration Management

Work Performance Reports – Physical or electronic representation of work performance information intended to generate decisions, actions or awareness. They are circulated to the stakeholders per the instructions in the communication mgmt. plan.

Change Control Tools – In order to facilitate configuration and change management, manual or automated tools may be used.

- **Configuration Control** – Focused on the specification of both the deliverables and processes.
- **Change Control** – Focused identifying, documenting, and approving or rejecting changes to the project documents, deliverables, or baselines.

Change Control Meetings – A change control board is responsible for meeting and reviewing the change requests and approving or rejecting those change requests.

1. All change control board decisions are documented and communicated to the stakeholders for information and follow up actions.
2. The status of all the changes approved or not, will be updated in the change request log as part of the project document updates.

Scope Management

Verified Deliverables – Completed and checked for correctness through control quality process.

Inspection – Tools and Techniques used to measure, examine, verify to determine whether work and deliverables meet requirements and product acceptance criteria.

Accepted Deliverables – When the acceptance criteria are formally signed off and approved by the customer or sponsor.

Cost Management

Earned Value Management (EVM)

- Commonly used method of performance measurement.
- It integrates project scope, cost and schedule measures to help project management team assess and measure project performance and progress.
- Develops and monitors three key dimensions of each work package and control account. These are Planned Value (PV), Earned Value (EV) and Actual Cost (AC).

Quality Management

Testing/Product Evaluations – Conducted to provide objective information about the quality of the product or service under test in accordance with the project requirements.

Technical Performance Analysis – compare technical accomplishments during project execution to the schedule of technical achievement.

Notes

Procurement Management

Audits – type of audit that may be used to consider the effectiveness of the risk management process.

- Claims Administration
- A claim is an assertion that the buyer did something that has hurt the seller and the seller asking for compensation.
- Changes that cannot be agreed upon are called contested changes.
- Contested changes usually involve a disagreement about the compensation to the vendor for implementing the change.
- Contested changes are also known as disputes, claims, or appeals. These can be settled directly between the parties themselves, through the court system, or by a process called arbitration.
- Inspections – Structured review of the work being performed by the contractor.
- Closed Procurements
- The buyer, usually through its authorized procurement administrator, provides the seller with formal written notice that the contract has been completed.
- Requirements for formal procurement closure are usually defined in the terms and conditions of the contract and are included in the procurement management plan.

Closing

Process of finalizing all activities for the project, phase, or contract.

- Obtain final acceptance of the project deliverables from relevant stakeholders in order to confirm that project scope and deliverables were achieved.
- Transfer the ownership of deliverables to the assigned stakeholders in accordance with the project plan in order to facilitate project closure.
- Obtain financial, legal, and administrative closure using generally accepted practices and policies in order to communicate formal project closure and ensure transfer of liability.
- Prepare and share the final project report according to the communications management plan in order to document and convey project performance and assist in project evaluation.
- Collate lessons learned that were documented throughout the project and conduct a comprehensive project review in order to update the organization's knowledge base.
- Archive project documents and materials using generally accepted practices in order to comply with statutory requirements and for potential use in future projects and audits.
- Obtain feedback from relevant stakeholders using appropriate tools and techniques and based on the stakeholder management plan in order to evaluate their satisfaction.
- Knowledge and Skills:
- Archiving practices and statutes
- Compliance (statute/organization)
- Contract closure requirements
- Close-out procedures
- Feedback techniques
- Performance measurement techniques (KPI and key success factors)
- Project review techniques
- Transition planning technique

Integration Management

- **Final Product, Service, or Result Transition** – Handing over to a different group or organization that will operate, maintain, and support it throughout its life cycle.

- **Final Report** – Summary of the project performance.

Notes

Table 7. Closing Process Group ITTO Matrix

Knowledge Area	Process	Inputs	Tools and Techniques	Outputs
Integration Management	**Close Project or Phase** The process of finalizing all activities across all the Project Management Process Groups to formally complete the project or phase.	1. Project Charter 2. Project Management Plan [*All Components*] 3. Project Documents [*Assumption Log, Basis of Estimates, Change Log, Lesson Learned Register, Milestone List, Project Communications, Quality Control Measurements, Quality Reports, Requirements Documentation, Risk Register, Risk Report*] 4. Accepted Deliverables 5. Business Documents 6. Agreements 7. Procurement Documentations 8. Organizational Process Assets	1. Expert Judgement 2. Data Analysis [*Document Analysis, Regression Analysis, Trend Analysis, Variance Analysis*] 3. Meetings	1. Project Document Updates [*Lessons Learned Register*] 2. Final Product, Service or Result Transition 3. Final Report 4. Organizational process assets updates

Earned Value Management Formulas

Planned Value (PV)
Value of work planned. Planned cost of value of the work to be done until this point in time.

Earned Value (EV)
Sum of the planned value of the completed work.
The value of the work accomplished until this point in time.

Actual Cost (AC)
The realized cost incurred for the work performed on an activity during a specific time period. The costs actually incurred to complete the work till this point in time.

Budget at Completion (BAC)
Project Baseline
The total planned value or budget for completing the entire project.

Schedule Variance (SV)
SV = EV − PV
Difference between the scheduled completion and actual completion of an activity or group of activities.
Negative SV is behind schedule; Positive SV is ahead of schedule.

Cost Variance (CV)
CV = EV − AC
Difference between the budgeted cost of completing an activity/group of activities and the actual budget spent for it. Negative CV: is over budget. Positive CV: is under budget.

Schedule Performance Index (SPI)
EV/PV
The measure of efficiency in managing the project's schedule. SPI > 1 is good (ahead of schedule)
= 1 on target
< 1 poor (behind schedule)

Cost Performance Index (CPI)
EV/AC
The measure of efficiency in managing the projects budget. CPI > 1 is good (under budget)
= 1 is on target
<1 is poor (over budget)

Estimate at Completion (EAC)
BAC/Cumulative CPI
This formula is used when ETC work i.e. remaining work is predicted to be performed at the cumulative CPI. This assumes the to date CPI will continue in future

Estimate at Completion (EAC)
AC + (BAC − EV)
This formula is used with remaining work is predicated to be performed exactly as per the original budget. Assumes any variances till date – both favorable and unfavorable - will not continue in future.

Estimate at Completion (EAC)
AC + Bottom-up ETC
This formula is used when new detailed bottom-up estimates are developed for the remaining work.

Estimate at Completion (EAC)
$EAC = AC + [(BAC - EV)/(cumulative\ CPI\ x\ cumulative\ SPI)]$
This formula is used when both cost and schedule performance indices are considered for performing remaining work. Most useful when project schedule impacts ETC effort. CV is assumed to be negative.

Estimate to Complete (ETC)
$ETC = EAC - AC$
This formula is used when work is proceeding as planned; ETC=Re-estimate (re-estimate the remaining work from the bottom up). How much more we expect project to cost from this point in time.

Variance at Completion (VAC)
$VAC = BAC - EAC$
How much under budget or over budget we expect the project to be once it is completed.

To-Complete Performance Index (TCPI)
$TCPI = (BAC - EV)/ (BAC - AC); TCPI= (BAC - EV)/ (EAC - AC)$
The cost performance needed in project for remaining work to stay within the planned budget (BAC) or the estimate at completion (EAC). Is the ratio of "work is remaining" to "funds are remaining"?

Communication Channels
$[n(n-1)]/2$
Communication channels between people; N = number of people involved.

Point of Total Assumption (PTA)
(Ceiling price - Target price)/Buyer's share ratio] + Target cost
- Price: The amount charged to buyer by seller (contractor)
- Target cost: Expected cost for doing the work at time of signing the contract
- Target fee: Sellers planned profit margin or fee for doing the work. Will be increased/ decreased using the Share ration based on performance
- Target Price: Target cost + target fee
- Share ratio: Ratio by which Buyer/Seller will share cost savings and cost overruns
- Ceiling Price: The maximum amount the buyer will pay for the contract irrespective of the costs.
- Actual Cost: Costs that actually incurred at end of contract

Notes

MASTERING THE PMP® EXAM [TOTAL PREP]

Expected Monetary Value (EMV)

Probability × Impact

A statistical concept that calculates the average outcome when the future includes scenarios that may or may not happen. Calculated by multiplying the value of each possible outcome by its probability of occurrence and adding them together. An EMV analysis is usually mapped out using a decision tree to represent the different options or scenarios. Used in *Perform Quantitative Analysis*

Three Point Estimate

P + (4M) + O/6

Where **P** is the Most Pessimistic Time; **M** is the Most Likely Time; **O** is the Most Optimistic Time for an activity.

Activity Variance σ2

[(P – O)/6]2

Where **P** is the Most Pessimistic Time; **O** is the Most Optimistic Time for an activity

Activity Standard Deviation SD (σ)

(P – O)/6

Where **P** is the Most Pessimistic Time; **O** is the Most Optimistic Time for an activity

ADV Consultants

PMP® Workbook
Games and Exercises
PMBOK Guide 6th Edition

Introduction

Matching

Match the definitions on the left with the correct term on the right.

1. A temporary endeavor to create a unique product, service or result. Project Life Cycle
2. On-going repetitive process Stakeholder
3. A set of related projects that have a common outcome Project Management
4. Projects, programs, sub programs grouped together that benefit the organization's investment strategy Sponsor
5. Someone that is positively or negatively affected by the project Program
6. Funds and approves the project Portfolio
7. Phases that the project goes through from beginning to closing Project
8. Application of knowledge, skills, tools, and techniques to project activities to meet the project requirements. Operations

Fill in the Blanks

Complete the following sentences with one of the terms in the box.

Project Team	Functional Manager	Projectized
Project Coordinator	Project Expeditor	Balanced Matrix
Functional Organization	Project Management Office	Project Manager

1. The _____ is responsible for assisting with planning and executing the work needed to produce the deliverables.
2. _____ is the group or department within a business, agency, or enterprise that defines and maintains standards for project management within the organization.

MASTERING THE PMP® EXAM [TOTAL PREP]

3. _____ is divided into specialized groups.
4. The _____ has power to make some decisions, have some authority, and report to a higher-level manager. His/her role is within a weak matrix.
5. The _____ acts as a staff assistant or communicator and doesn't have power to make any decisions. His/her role is within a weak matrix.
6. A _____ organization is divided by projects and the PM has full control of the projects.
7. In an _____ environment the power is shared between the functional and project manager.
8. _____ is the person responsible to ensure the project meets its objective as planned.
9. _____ is the head of a specialized department in the organization.

Memorization

1. Any item either internal or external to the project, which is required by the process before that process proceeds.
2. Defining a new project or a new phase of an existing project at a high level to obtain authorization to start.
3. Putting the project in a cohesive whole.
4. Something tangible or a defined systematic procedure employed by a human resource used in performing an activity to produce a product or result.
5. A product, result, or service generated by a process. May be an input to a successor process.
6. Consist of 24 processes that establish the scope, objectives and define the course of action the team will take to successfully complete the project.
7. Consist of the processes that track, review, and regulate the progress and performance of the project against the plan. Identify any changes to the plan and initiate the corresponding changes.
8. Consist of the process to formally complete, close the project, phase, or contract.

9. Consist of 10 processes that the project team members complete according to the plan to satisfy the project requirements.
10. Updated procedures, guidelines, templates, lessons learned, etc.
11. Project progress data that has been analyzed through the monitoring and controlling processes.

Matching

1. Putting the project in a cohesive whole.   Stakeholder Management
2. Ensures the project includes all the work required, and only the work required, to complete the project successfully.   Procurement Management
3. Creating and managing the timely completion of the project.   Cost Mgmt.
4. Acquiring and managing the resources needed to successfully complete the project.   Communications Management
5. The degree to which the project fulfils requirements.   Schedule Management
6. Creating and managing the approved time phase budget.   Scope Management
7. Ensure timely & appropriate generation collection, distribution, storage, retrieval, & ultimate disposition of project information   Integration Management
8. Identify people, groups or organizations that could impact or be impacted   Resource Management
9. Working to increase the probability and impact of opportunities on the project (positive events), while decreasing the probability and impact of threats to the project (negative events).   Risk Management
10. The processes necessary to purchase or acquire products, services or results needed from outside the project team.   Quality Management

Notes

Crossword Puzzles

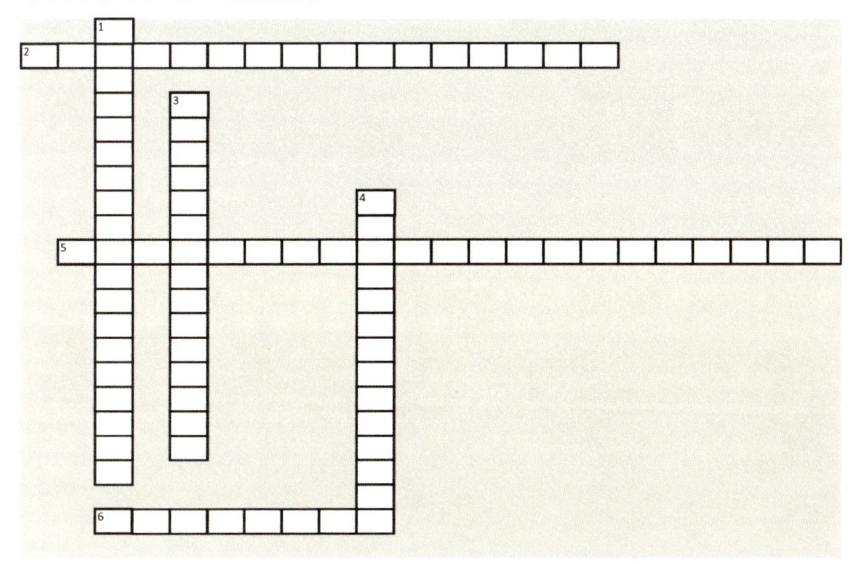

Across

2. Project artifacts created and updated in various processes (e.g., risk register, issue log, change log, etc.)
5. How to guide that describes how the project will be executed, monitored and controlled, and closed.
6. Interactive communication tool for the exchange or project information.

Down

1. Raw data collected during the executing process group to be used later to analyze the performance of the project.
3. Expertise provided by a group or individual with specialized knowledge or training.
4. Includes any scope changes, corrective actions, preventive.

MASTERING THE PMP® EXAM [TOTAL PREP]

Fill in the Blanks

1. Name the three (3) types of a PMO:

    a. _____

    b. _____

    c. _____

2. Name the three (3) Organizational Structures:

    a. _____

    b. _____

    c. _____

3. What are the two (2) roles a PM can have in a weak matrix:

    a. _____

    b. _____

4. What are three (3) project triggers:

    a. _____

    b. _____

    c. _____

Multiple Choice Questions

1. Portfolio Management is defined as:
   A. A group of related projects that have a common output.
   B. Adhering to the budget, schedule and scope of a project.
   C. A collection of projects, programs, and operations managed as a group to achieve strategic objectives of the organization.
   D. Follows a business process

2. A collection of generally sequential project phases whose name and number are determined by the control needs of the organization or organizations involved in the project. Sometimes an organization can document it with a methodology.
   A. Project Phases
   B. Agile
   C. Waterfall
   D. Project Life Cycle

3. "The application of Knowledge, skills, tools and techniques to project activities to meet the project requirements" is the definition of.
   A. Project Management Office
   B. Organizational Structures
   C. Project Management
   D. Program Management

4. Which of the following PMO structures plays a consulting role, e.g., supplying templates, best practices, training, computer information, and lessons learned from other projects?
   A. Directive
   B. Supporting
   C. Controlling
   D. None of the approve

Notes

5. Internal and external factors that influence a project's success which is not under the project team's control and inputs to most processes are referred to as:

    A. Enterprise Environmental Factors
    B. Organizational Process Assets
    C. Inputs
    D. Project Techniques

6. Sophia is managing a group of related or unrelated projects/programs to achieve a specific strategic business objective is referred to as:

    A. Program Manager
    B. Project Manager
    C. Portfolio Manager
    D. Stakeholder

7. Any and all process related assets plans, policies, procedures, guidelines historical information and lessons learned an organization has is referred to:

    A. Organizational Process Assets
    B. Enterprise Environmental Factors
    C. PMO
    D. Projects

8. The person responsible for the funding of the project and assisting the PM with ensuring unnecessary changes occur.

    A. Project Manager
    B. Senior Manager
    C. Sponsor
    D. Project Team

9. The PMO structure that provide support and require compliance, e.g., PM methodologies, specific templates-forms-tools, or conformance to governance. Control from this type of PMO is moderate is referred to as?

   A. Controlling
   B. Directive
   C. Supportive
   D. Balanced Matrix

10. The organizational structure where both the functional and project manager share responsibilities in resources, budget and managing the project is known as?

    A. Functional
    B. Balance Matrix
    C. Projectized
    D. Weak Matrix

Project Management Roles and Responsibilities

Fill-in the Blanks

Interactional	Transformational	Charismatic
Transactional	Technical Project Management	Servant Leader
Leadership	Laissez-Faire	Strategic and Business Management

1. List the three components of the PM triangle:

    a. _____

    b. _____

    c. _____

2. Allowing the team to make their own decisions and establish their own goals, also referred to as taking a hands-off style. _____

3. Focus on goals, feedback, and accomplishment to determine rewards; management by exception. _____

4. Demonstrates commitment to serve and put other people first; focuses on other people's growth, learning, development, autonomy, and well-being; concentrates on relationships, community and collaboration; leadership is secondary and emerges after service. _____

5. Empowering followers through idealized attributes and behaviors, inspirational motivation, encouragement for innovation and creativity, and individual consideration. _____

6. Able to inspire; is high-energy, enthusiastic, self-confident; holds strong convictions. _____

7. A combination of transactional, transformational, and charismatic. _____

Notes

Matching

1. Formal, Authoritative, Legitimate (e.g., formal position granted in the organization or team)   Reward-oriented

2. Respect or admiration others hold for the individual, credibility gained   Positional

3. Skill, information possessed; experience, training, education, certification   Punitive or Coercive Positional

4. Ability to give praise, (monetary or other desired items)   Referent

5. Ability to invoke discipline or negative consequences   Expert

6. Accepts others for what and who they are, shows open concern.   Social

7. Ability to understand and manage people.   Intellectual

8. Measure of management practice and potential.   Emotional

9. Ability to perceive emotions and the information they present and to manage them; measure of interpersonal skills.   Managerial

10. Measure of human intelligence over multiple aptitudes.   Authentic

Initiating

Matching

1. A document that provides the required info from a business standpoint to determine whether the project is worth the investment. — Project Charter

2. A document or communication that defines the initial intentions of a project (e.g., contract, memorandum of understanding (MOU), letters of agreement, verbal agreements, email, etc.) — Business Case

3. Project document used to record all assumptions and constraints — Agreements

4. Project document output from Identify Stakeholders that include the identification, assessment, and classification of identified stakeholders — Assumption log

5. Names the PM and formally authorizes him/her to expend resources to achieve project objectives and needs. It may include high-level requirements, risks, summary budget, milestone schedules, assumptions, and constraints, etc. — Stakeholder Register

6. Process that develops a document that formally authorizes a project or a phase and documenting initial requirements that satisfy the stakeholder's needs and expectations. — Identify Stakeholders

7. The process of identifying all people or organizations impacted by the project, and documenting relevant information regarding their interests, expectation, involvement, and influence on project success. — Develop Project Charter

Questions

1. The organization wants to expand its skin care line. Research and development have developed a new concept, and marketing advises that all efforts should be made to create and release this product as soon as possible. A business case has been created and accepted, and you have been named project manager for this effort. You are determining how you will proceed. All the following should be determined before project planning except?

    A. Business case
    B. Project scope statement
    C. Project stakeholders
    D. Project Charter

2. Which of the following statements is not true about operations?

    A. Operational work may be unrelated to any project within the organization
    B. Operational work may be the reason a project is begun
    C. Operational work may be the result of a project
    D. Operational work may be done only in the context of a project

3. Which of the following is done in the initiating process group?

    A. Work with the customer to determine acceptance criteria
    B. Recommend changes and defect repair
    C. Evaluate Risk Responses
    D. Update corporate processes and procedures based on lessons learned

4. Which of the following is not a project?

    A. Implementation of a new software program
    B. Design of a new housing development
    C. Assembly line in a car manufacturing
    D. Construction of a new building

Notes

5. You have just reviewed your performance on the project, and you realize you must take steps to improve your skills in managing stakeholders. All the following are responsibilities of the project manager in stakeholder management except:

    A. Figuring out when stakeholders will be involved in the project and how extensively

    B. Selecting the appropriate stakeholders for the project

    C. Ask stakeholders to let you know about problems in project communications and relationships

    D. Getting stakeholders' approval on final requirements

6. What are assumptions?

    A. Identified in project initiating, including in project planning, and managed throughout project executing

    B. Identified in project planning, validated in project planning, and used in project monitoring and controlling to create control limits

    C. Identified in project initiating, analyzed in project planning, and managed throughout the project

    D. Identified in project planning, used to make planning decisions, and managed throughout project monitoring and controlling

7. When is the project manager assigned?

    A. Project selection

    B. Initiating

    C. Integration

    D. Planning

8. You have been planning a project that will result in many changes to the Organization. Your team that will execute the project plan has been identified, and you expect to get approval to kick off the project soon. You've just learned that your project will impact the work of 600 employees that will not be involved in any aspect of your project. What is the best thing to do?

A. Modify your stakeholder engagement plan to include information sessions for the 600 people

B. Get the stakeholders' sign-off that the requirements have been finalized

C. Create a stakeholder engagement assessment matrix

D. Add the 600 people to the stakeholder register and interview them to assess their needs

9. There are two projects for the organization to choose between: Project A with an NPV of US $145,000 and Project B with an NPV of US $285,000. What is the opportunity cost of selecting project B?

A. $145,000

B. $85,000

C. $130,000

D. $40,000

10. Stakeholder register includes which of the following:

A. Role, major requirements, influence, and classification

B. Communication requirements

C. Level of interest, and engagement level

D. Stakeholder name, major requirements, and communication requirements

Planning

Matching

1. A narrative explanation of what the project entails includes the business need, scope description, and organization's strategic plan.   WBS Dictionary

2. Authorized, time-phased budget used to measure, monitor, and control cost performance of the project   Requirements Documentation

3. Contains the descriptions of the product or business process, business need, goals and objectives   Project Statement of Work

4. Additional information about work packages (e.g., description of work, responsible person, cost estimate)   Cost Baseline

5. Approximation cost to complete project activities   Requirements Management Plan

6. Comprehensive description of the project's deliverables and the work required to create those deliverables   Project Scope Statement

7. How requirements will be planned, tracked and reported.   Activity Cost Estimates

Matching

1. Define Activities   Scope Baseline
2. Create WBS   Activity List
3. Estimate Costs   Cost Baseline
4. Define Scope   Source Selection Criteria
5. Determine Budget   Activity Cost Estimate
6. Plan Procurement   Project Scope Statement

Notes

MASTERING THE PMP® EXAM [TOTAL PREP]

Fill-in the Blanks

Create WBS	Cost of Quality	Parametric Estimating
Funding Limit Reconciliation	Bottom Up Estimating	Analogous Estimating
Resource Smoothing	Lag Decomposition	Lead

1. The process where all project work is sub-divided and broken down to the work package level _____

2. The technique where work packages are broken down to activities _____

3. Starting an activity prior to completing the preceding activity _____

4. Delaying an activity's start date _____

5. Using a similar prior project to estimate activity durations or cost _____

6. Using a statistical relationship to estimate cost or duration _____

7. Breaking down an activity into smaller component to make a very accurate estimate _____

8. Adjusting the level of resources when resources have been over-allocated, without allowing the schedule to slip _____

9. Adjustments made to project expenditure to account f or funding limits _____

10. Cost of conformance and non-conformance _____

117

MASTERING THE PMP® EXAM [TOTAL PREP]

Fill-in the blanks

1. The two (2) schedule compression techniques are:
   _____
   _____

2. The lowest level of the WBS is:
   _____

3. Strategies for negative risk (threat):
   _____
   _____
   _____
   _____

4. Strategies for positive risk (opportunities):
   _____
   _____
   _____
   _____

5. Requirements of a contract:
   _____
   _____
   _____
   _____

6. The three (3) main types of contracts are:
   _____
   _____
   _____

7. The three (3) Communication Methods are:

   _____
   _____
   _____

8. Three (3) types of communication:

   _____
   _____
   _____

Questions

1. The main objectives of the processes in Planning are?

   A. Determine the actions that must be taken to meet project objectives define project scope and refine project objectives.

   B. Identify project stakeholders and authorize the project to start.

   C. Acquire resources

   D. Test the product

2. How does planning fit into the project life cycle?

   A. Once Direct and Manage Project work begins plans cannot change.

   B. Project plans are updated as new information becomes available throughout a project.

   C. Detailed planning accounts for possible changes making it unlikely that plans will have to be revised later in the project life cycle.

   D. Project plans are changed at every stage of the process.

Notes

MASTERING THE PMP® EXAM [TOTAL PREP]

Fill in the Story

Complete the sentences with the correct process or ITTO.

The Project Charter and Stakeholder register has been created. The project team is assembled to dietermine the project management approach for the project. What process in the PM in ¹ _____. The output is the ²· _____ which defines how the project will be executed, monitored, controlled and closed.

In order to determine what the project needs to accomplish; the PM and the project team must meet with the stakeholders and perform the ³· _____ process using the five data gathering techniques ⁴· _____, ⁵· _____, ⁶ _____, ⁷· _____, and ⁸· _____. The gathered information will then be in ⁹· _____ which is the project document output of the process.

The output is then used in the ¹⁰· _____ process that develops a detailed description of the project and product. The document called ¹¹· _____ also documents the acceptance criteria of the project. From this document, the PM and project team will break down the project deliverables using the ¹²· _____ technique to create ¹³· _____ which will facilitate better planning and tracking of project work. The details of this document will be further explained in the ¹⁴· _____. All three components are referred to the scope baseline which will reside in the project management plan.

The PM and project team will further decompose the work package items from the WBS in order to get a more detailed, granular description of all the work to be done, which is called a ¹⁵· _____ the PM is in the ¹⁶· _____ process. Once it's completed, the PM will move on to ¹⁷· _____, which involves determining the logical order of the activities based on any dependencies, the output of this process is ¹⁸· _____. Upon completion of the process the

MASTERING THE PMP® EXAM [TOTAL PREP]

PM and team can estimate the number of work periods needed to complete each activity in the [19.] _____ process. The PM and team have their estimates and are now ready to complete the [20] _____ process. The output [21.] _____ which will be approved by the sponsor and management will reside in the project management plan to serve as the basis of measuring actual schedule performance.

The PM and team are ready now to create a budget, they must first create a [22.] _____ in which it serves as a how to guide on the overall methods and standards that will be utilized in establishing and controlling their budget. They will then move on to [23] _____, using the [24] _____, [25] _____, or [26] _____ techniques. Then the team will be ready to aggregate all these items via the [27] _____ process to come up with the [28] _____. Which will reside in the project management plan and serve as the basis of measuring actual cost performance.

For the team to ensure they are producing quality deliverables is to prepare a [29.] _____, in which they will identify their overall approach to follow in terms of ensuring the quality of our work, which will include certain processes and methodologies, we will follow. As part of this effort, they will also produce [30.] _____, which provide an objective way to test certain aspects of the deliverables. Another goal of this process is to identify those processes they will perform most frequently and determine how they can make them more efficient. The results of the analysis will be outlined in the [31.] _____, which is another output of Plan Quality Management.

Now the team is ready to outline the resources needed for a successful project, they are in the [32.] _____ process to produce a [33.] _____. The PM will also produce the [34.] _____ that clarifies team direction while establishing boundaries. The PM and team are now estimating team resources and the type and quantities of materials, equipment, and supplies necessary to perform project work, they are in the [35.] _____ process.

The PM and team realize it is important to develop an appropriate approach and plan for how project information will be compiled, stored and disseminated based on the stakeholder's needs and requirements, they are in the ^36._____ process.

The PM and team are ready to work on a plan for identifying, evaluating and handling risk, and this is laid out in the ^37._____.
Once the outline has been completed on how risk will be managed, they will perform the ^38._____, process which involves identifying specific risks the project faces. We will document this information in the ^39._____. Now the team is ready to analyze the risks to prioritize them according to their likelihood of occurrence, likely impact, and how far off in time they are. They are in the ^40._____ process. The results can be viewed in a ^41._____. Non-critical risks are noted on the ^42._____, meaning the team does not act right away but will instead track the items to ensure they do not become more significant during the monitor risk process.

The next step the team can skip but it involves numerically analyzing the effect of the various risks on project impacts such as cost, schedule, etc. This process is called ^43._____. The technique that is used in this process is ^44._____.

In terms of acquisitions, the team will determine using the ^45._____ technique if they need to go outside for a service or equipment. They will develop an approach towards handling the acquisition, which includes things like what items must be procured and when, which types of sellers they prefer to work with, and what types of contracts they will want to use. The information will be documented in the ^46._____, which will guide their procurement efforts throughout the project.

In managing the stakeholders, the team will develop management strategies to engage stakeholders throughout the project life cycle, based on the analysis of their needs, interests, and impact on project success. This will be documented in the ^47._____.

Notes

MASTERING THE PMP® EXAM [TOTAL PREP]

Put in Order

Place the processes in the box into the correct planning order.

Develop Project Management Plan	Estimate Costs	Determine Budget	Estimate Activity Durations	Estimate Activity Resources	Determine Budget
Plan Scope Management Plan	Plan Cost Management Plan	Plan Schedule Management Plan	Plan Quality Management Plan	Plan Resource Management Plan	Plan Risk Management Plan
Plan Communications Management Plan	Plan Stakeholder Management Plan	Plan Procurement Management Plan	Plan Risk Responses	Define Scope	Create WBS
Perform Quantitative Risk Analysis	Perform Qualitative Risk Analysis	Identify Risks	Collect Requirements	Define Activities	Sequence Activities

1.	9.	17.
2.	10.	18.
3.	11.	19.
4.	12.	20.
5.	13.	21.
6.	14.	22.
7.	15.	23.
8.	16.	24.

Matching

1. Comparing actuals or planned products, processes, and practices to those of comparable organizations to identify best practices, generate ideas of improvement, and provide a basis for measuring performance.   Interviews

2. A checklist is a list of steps to be carried out for an activity. The list is made as comprehensive as possible so that this becomes the tool to verify that all the required steps for a quality item is carried out without missing any one of them.   Benchmarking

3. Also known as Tally Sheets used for gathering data, organizing facts, and collecting attribute data during inspections.   Focus Groups

4. Talking to stakeholder directly to gather information about a specific product or requirement.   Check Sheets

5. Bringing together prequalified stakeholders and subject matter experts to learn about their expectations about a proposed product. A trained moderator guides the group through an interactive discussion designed to be more conversational than a one on one interview.   Statistical Samplings

6. Gathering information from different sources like online reviews and conferences to identify the market trend and market capabilities. It refines the procurement objectives of the project management team to leverage the mature technologies, processes and organizations. It also balances the risks that are associated with the vendors who provide the services or materials needed for the project.   Questionnaires and Surveys

7. Selecting a portion of the population to test, testing the whole population would be time consuming and costly.   Brain Storming

8. Gather information from stakeholders by sending out written questions.	Market Research
9. Used in a group environment, led by a facilitator it is a technique to gather ideas in a short period of time. The participants generate ideas and then analyze them.	Check Lists

Questions

1. Jennifer the project manager was informed midway through project planning that she was given inaccurate data regarding new regulations affecting the required end date of her project. She may need to make a few adjustments, but she thinks she can still manage the project to complete it before the regulations take effect. She confirms this by analyzing the sequence of activities with the least amount of scheduling flexibility. Which of the following techniques is she using?

    A. Bottom up
    B. Precedence diagramming
    C. Critical path method
    D. Flowchart

2. James is gathering data with the team to determine how various factors might be linked to potential problems. In which of the following quality management process is the project manager working?

    A. Control Quality
    B. Plan Quality Management
    C. Quality Analysis
    D. Manage Quality

3. You are a project manager for a US $2,000,000 website development project. Your project is 50 percent into project executing and remains on time, on budget, and on specification. This morning your project sponsor called to express concern about the project. Based on the schedule baseline, the project should

Notes

be nearing implementation, but the sponsor does not know the current status of the project. You remind the sponsor that your team produces a detailed status report weekly and distributes it via email. The sponsor says email is too impersonal and verbal updates are preferred. This situation suggests problems with which of the following project management processes?

    A. Plan Communications Management
    B. Control Communications
    C. Quality Management
    D. Plan Stakeholder Engagement

4. Sophia has completed the WBS, estimates for each work package, and the network diagram are completed. The next thing for her to work on is:

    A. Estimate Resource Durations
    B. Collect Requirements
    C. Sequence Activities
    D. Develop Schedule

5. The project manager and her team are working with cost estimates, the resource management plan, and the project schedule to determine a cost baseline for your project. Which process group are you in?

    A. Closing
    B. Executing
    C. Initiating
    D. Planning

6. Once the charter has been signed, what is the next thing to start?

    A. Begin to complete work packages
    B. Start integrated change control
    C. Validate scope
    D. Start to create management plans

7. When would a team use SWOT analysis?

    A. Identifying risks

    B. Calculating the cost benefit analysis

    C. Creating WBS

    D. Verifying scope

8. During the first half of a software development project, three developers left for other projects without being replaced, two additional team members went on vacation without informing the project manager. What did the project manager not do correctly?

    A. Communications management plan

    B. Responsibility assignment matrix

    C. Resource histogram

    D. Resource management plan

9. Which of the following is part of the Project Management Plan?

    A. Risk register

    B. Baselines

    C. Lessons learned

    D. Milestone list

10. You are leading the construction of a new office building. The project sponsor asks you to email him a project document that was presented during the last project status meeting. The project sponsor states that he has forgotten the name of the document, but he remembers it contained the description, owner, source, priority, and status of product requirements. Which project document is the project sponsor requesting?

    A. The requirements management plan

    B. The scope management plan

    C. The work breakdown structure (WBS)

    D. Requirements Traceability Matrix

Executing

Matching

1. Any product, service or result required to complete a project.   Lessons Learned Document

2. Project document where all issues that are negatively affecting the project are recorded and tracked.   Deliverable

3. Any project request that is submitted to whatever change control board or decision-making group to be reviewed for approval or denial.   Issue Log

4. Document what went well and what didn't throughout the project lifecycle. Used a reference for future projects.   Change Request

Fill in the Story

The process in which the team executes the plans and produces the deliverables is called 1. _____. In this process, the team relies on the 2. _____, which will help them keep track of all project information, documents and plans, and help facilitate effective communications. The team will be looking for ways to prevent failures from occurring, this is called 3. _____. 4. _____, is when a problem has been identified, and the project's goal is to bring future performance back in line with the project management plan. While the work is being performed the team gathers a lot of information in raw form, such as percent complete, time and money spent, etc. This information does not consider planned values is called 5. _____.

6. _____ process of using existing knowledge and creating new knowledge to achieve the project's objectives and contribute to organizational learning. While the work is being performed the team with the help of the stakeholders document

Notes

MASTERING THE PMP® EXAM [TOTAL PREP]

factors that lead to the success and failures of the project is called
7. _____ it is also an output of this process.

Auditing the quality of deliverables to ensure the quality management plan is being adhered to is the process of
8. _____. This process also involves implementing the steps the team planned in 9. _____
to help increase efficiency in the organization.

The PM negotiates with the functional managers based on what was identified in the Resource Management plan to bring on resources with the correct skill set to successfully accomplish the project deliverables, the PM is in 10. _____ process. Now that the PM has brought on the team members, he/she is using team building activities to develop the team to ensure decreased turnover, improved individual skills and improved team. The team building activity theory is called 11. _____. The key output of this process which are evaluations conducted to gauge a team's effectiveness is called 12. _____.

Now the team has been developed, the PM continues to track team member performance, providing feedback, resolving issues, and managing team changes to optimize project performance. This is done via the 13. _____ process and utilizes tools such as conflict management. The favorable conflict management technique that incorporates multiple viewpoints and insights from different perspective and requires a cooperative attitude and open dialogue is 14. _____.

Ensures an efficient and effective information flow between the project team and the stakeholders using technologies and methods per the communication management plan. The PM is in the
15. _____ process. The main output of this process is
16. _____.

In order to successfully complete a required deliverable, the PM needs to acquire services from outside the organization. The make and buy analysis have been completed along with all the plans needed to select a qualified seller. The PM must now choose the qualified seller who will complete the work as per the contract for a completion of a successfully project. The PM is the [17] _____ process, and a key technique he/she can use is [18] _____. The main output of this process is [19] _____.

During project execution the PM realizes she/he needs to proceed with the backup plan put in place during planning. The PM is the [20] _____ process, which implements agreed upon risk strategies to minimize the threats to the delivery of the deliverable in terms of time, cost or quality.

The PM is communicating and working with stakeholders to meet their needs, address issues as they occur, and foster stakeholder engagement in project activities throughout the project life cycle. The process the PM is in [21] _____ which objective is to increase the likelihood of project success by ensuring the stakeholders clearly understand project goals, objectives, benefits, and risk.

MASTERING THE PMP® EXAM [TOTAL PREP]

Questions

1. You are managing a project to update the packaging and digital media for a popular kid's toy to promote a charity fundraiser. The project is well underway, and you are currently actively collecting and storing information about each deliverable team's progress, creating forecasts for your sponsor, distributing work performance reports and planning presentations to key stakeholders, and verifying delivery. Which process are you performing?

    A. Monitor Communications

    B. Manage Stakeholder Engagement

    C. Plan Communications Management

    D. Manage Communications

2. Sonia has recently been assigned to lead a project that is halfway into execution. The project has many stakeholders, and she's trying to determine how to engage them effectively. Which of the following will best help her in this effort?

    A. Project management plan

    B. Project charter

    C. Work performance reports

    D. Procurement documents

3. At the start of project execution, a project manager needs to acquire the development team. However, the functional manager indicates that of those developers who were planned for the project, one is unavailable as she is currently completing another project. What should the project manager do to understand the proposed team member's future availability?

    A. Contact the team member's functional manager

    B. Review the resource requirements

    C. Examine the resource breakdown structure

    D. Look at the resource calendar

4. Susan has allowed her project team the use of flextime where project team members may take time off during regular business

Notes

hours and make up the time during the evening hours or weekends. Recently, excessive use of flextime has become a roadblock as some team members are not available when needed. The project team feels they should set a standard that flextime is only to be used for personal emergencies. How should Susan handle this situation?

    A. Contact the human resources department to update the corporate policies to prohibit flextime

    B. Submit a change request to update the team charter based on the team's inputs

    C. Discuss the issue with the team and update the team charter accordingly

    D. Do nothing as the team has already agreed to use flextime for personal emergencies only

5. You are leading a project team with a software application upgrade project within a project-oriented organizational structure. You were recently informed that one of your project team members falsified required certifications on their resume', and you have verified the information as accurate. You want to terminate the team member's employment. What should you do first?

    A. Contact the functional manager

    B. Review the resource management plan

    C. Immediately terminate the employee for cause

    D. Review the enterprise environmental factors

6. The updated version of the product is to be at the customer's location by the end of the week, but your team realizes they will be unable to complete the deliverable by then. You have sat with the team to look for solutions to resolve this issue but there is nothing to be done for missing the deadline. The deployment team who is supposed to install the product at the customer site is under a lot of stress to meet their deadline and is going to be furious that the update will not be there at the end of the week. What is the best action for you currently?

A. Ignore the issue and wait until the deadline hoping the team eventually makes it
B. Send the status report to the customer
C. Call the customer to inform him/her via phone of the delay
D. Add more resources to the task

7. What is the output of Conduct Procurements?
    A. Bidder Conferences
    B. Select Sellers
    C. Risk Register
    D. Procurement Management Plan

8. Lessons Learned register is the output of which of the following processes?
    A. Manage Knowledge
    B. Direct and Manage Project Work
    C. Close Project/Phase
    D. Collect Requirements

9. Which process has the objective of communicating and working with stakeholders to meet their needs and expectations, addresses issues and foster appropriate stakeholder involvement?
    A. Manage Stakeholder Engagement
    B. Manage Communications
    C. Control Communications
    D. Monitor Stakeholder Engagement

10. Sean has just left his program manager's office after an attempt to get additional people for his team. His program manager told him that everyone was working at maximum and there were no other internal resources for use. He also told Jose to take the appropriate action to correct the issue. What should Sean do next?

A. Submit a change request and evaluate the cost impact of external resource acquisition.

B. Speak directly to his peers to see if they can share some resources.

C. Provide overtime incentive to his existing team.

D. Escalate to his project sponsor.

Monitoring & Controlling

Matching

1. Evaluating identified options in order to select the options or approaches to use to execute and perform the work of the project. — Earned Value Analysis

2. Provides an integrated perspective on scope, schedule, and cost performance. — Performance Reviews

3. Tracks the work that remains to be completed in the iteration backlog. Used to analyze the variance with respect to an ideal burndown based on the work committed from iteration planning. — Trend Analysis

4. To measure, compare, and analyze schedule performance against the schedule baseline such as actual start and finish dates, percent complete, and remaining duration for work in progress. — Alternate Analysis

5. To determine the essential features and relationships of components in the PMP to establish a reserve for the schedule duration, budget, estimated cost, or funds for a project. — Root Cause Analysis

6. Used to determine the basic underlying reason that causes a variance or a defect or a risk. — Stakeholder Analysis

Notes

7.	Systematically gathering and analyzing quantitative and qualitative information to determine whose interests should be considered throughout the project.	Technical Performance Analysis
8.	Using mathematical models to forecast future outcomes based on historical results.	Variance Analysis
9.	Determining the cause and degree of difference between the baseline and actual performance.	Reserve Analysis
10.	Comparing technical accomplishments during project execution to the schedule of technical achievement.	Iteration Burndown Charts

MASTERING THE PMP® EXAM [TOTAL PREP]

Fill in the story

Complete the sentences to test your knowledge on processes and ITTOs.

The process where the team is examining the overall project work and comparing the actual results to the planned results, while also identifying preventive and/or corrective actions to be taken, is called ¹·_____, the main input used during this process is called ²·_____. Along the process if it is determined a change needs to be made the PM must invoke the ³·_____ process, the project document output of this process is called ⁴·_____.

The PM regularly meets with the key stakeholder/sponsor to bring objectivity to the acceptance process and increase the probability of the final product, service, or result acceptance by validating each deliverable, the process is called ⁵·_____. The PM uses ⁶·_____ technique to measure and examine the deliverable, to determine whether the work meets the requirements and product acceptance criteria set in the project scope statement. The result is the ⁷·_____ as the output.

The PM is managing the activity progress and managing changes to the schedule baseline, the process is called ⁸·_____. Using earned value techniques, the PM wants to predict the future, ⁹·_____ is the output of this process utilizing the technique.

Using ¹⁰·_____ which are projected expenditures plus anticipated liabilities as input, the PM is managing the progress and any changes to the cost baseline. The PM is in the ¹¹·_____ process using various tools and techniques to produce ¹²·_____ on how the project work is performing compared to the cost baseline.

The process that can be worked in parallel with the Validated Scope Process to ensure project deliverables and work meet the requirements specified by key stakeholders for final acceptance is called ¹³·_____. This process is concerned with the

14. _____ of the deliverables. The main output of this process is 15. _____.

Once the project has procurement contracts in place, the PM needs to oversee the relationship and ensure that the seller is meeting their obligations. The PM does this via the 16. _____ process. There are three specific tools used by the PM or team to oversee this process, the tools are 17. _____, 18. _____ and 19. _____. The main output of this process is 20. _____, which is a structured way of reviewing the sellers' performance relative to its contractual obligations.

The process by which the PM implements the agreed-upon risk response plans, tracks identified risks, identifies and analyzes new risks, and evaluates risk process effectiveness throughout the project is called 21. _____. The two data analysis techniques used in this process are 22. _____ and 23. _____.

The PM spends 90 percent of his/her time on communications. In a well-run project the PM and team ensure the information needs of the project stakeholders are met throughout the entire project life cycle. The PM is in the 24. _____ process using 25. _____ and 26. _____ techniques.

The PM is using interpersonal and team skills to monitor overall project stakeholder relationships and adjust strategies and plans for engaging stakeholders. This process will increase the efficiency and effectiveness of engaging stakeholders as the project evolves. The PM is in which process 27. _____.

Notes

Questions

1. A change request has just been received from the customer that does not affect the project schedule and is easy to complete. What should you as the project manager do first?

    A. Contact the project sponsor for permission
    B. Implement the change
    C. Evaluate the impacts on other project constraints
    D. Perform the integrated change control

2. If earned value (EV) = 350, actual cost (AC) = 400, and planned value (PV) = 325, what is the cost variance (CV)?

    A. 400
    B. 350
    C. -75
    D. -50

3. Your project has run into cost difficulties. The project scope must be completed, but at less cost. As a project manager what option could you use?

    A. Perform Earned Value Management
    B. Perform a value analysis
    C. Recover some sunk costs
    D. Remove team members

4. You have a contract stating that the seller must submit monthly acceptance tests to the project manager. If the seller does not submit such acceptance tests, the seller is:

    A. In breach of contract
    B. Is not in violation
    C. Not following the procurement management plan
    D. Can decide to submit the report or not

5. What does estimate at completion (EAC) mean?
   A. Anticipated total cost at project completion
   B. Actual cost at completion
   C. Cost performance
   D. Work to be completed

6. A technical defect was identified in a deliverable that is due to the customer today. The project manager knows the customer does not have the technical understanding to notice the defect. The deliverable meets the contract requirements, but it does not meet the project manager's quality standard. What should the project manager do in this situation?
   A. Ignore it
   B. Inform the customer of the issue
   C. Document in lesson learned for future reference
   D. Obtain final approval from the customer

7. What process group is the Validate Scope process in?
   A. Executing
   B. Monitoring and controlling
   C. Planning
   D. Closing

8. Your team member lets you know an activity on the schedule has been delayed. What is the first thing you should do?
   A. Crash or fast track
   B. Use contingency reserves
   C. Report to management
   D. Determine how much of a problem it is

9. You receive a call from a team member notifying you that there is a variance between the speed of a system on the project and the desired or planned speed. You're surprised because that performance measurement was not identified in planning. You are

evaluating whether the variance warrants a response, in which part of the project management process are you?

- A. Executing
- B. Monitoring and controlling
- C. Closing
- D. Initiating

10. A project manager discovers a work package has been completed for substantially less cost than planned. Which of the following is not among the first things to consider doing?

    - A. Make sure all the work was done
    - B. Make sure the right resources were used
    - C. Make sure all project processes were followed
    - D. Identify ways to increase the result.

Notes

Closing

Fill-in the Story

Upon closing of the project or phase the PM must ensure that the deliverables have been properly 1. _____.
The PM will gather the inputs from the stakeholders citing what went well and could improve the next time and update the 2. _____ document. The document will be archived in the organizational process assets to be helpful on future projects. The PM will then release the team members per the 3. _____. Finally, the PM ensures the deliverables are properly transitioned and issue a report to the stakeholders that the project has been closed.

Questions

1. Your project just came to an end; the team is breathing a sigh of relief. None of them were confident the project would meet the end date. Which of the following is not a reason why the project was having difficulty?

    A. Lack of a payback period

    B. Lack of a communications management plan

    C. Lack of a staffing management plan

    D. Lack of milestones

2. Your website development project has progressed according to plan and coming to an end. Your team is excited about the product they have created. Now they are looking ahead to finding new projects to work on. You caution them that the current project cannot be considered complete until after the closing process group. Closure includes all the following except:

    A. Updating the company's organizational process assets

    B. Determining performance measures

    C. Turning over the product of the project

    D. Documenting the degree to which each project phase was properly closed after its completion

3. Why is performance reporting important during administrative closure?

   A. Gain approval to start the lessons learned
   B. Communicate the team's success
   C. Prove formal acceptance has been achieved
   D. Show progress made on activities

4. Which is an output of the Close Project or Phase process?

   A. A project management plan
   B. Project archives
   C. A risk management plan
   D. A project charter

5. You have completed your project and sent the final deliverable to the customer, but the customer refuses to give final acceptance of the project. It is most important for the project manager to:

   A. Let the CEO of the company know
   B. Call a lawyer
   C. Document the issue
   D. Tell the functional manager

6. Project managers will create and accumulate several documents during each of their project's phases. Some of these will be completed early and won't be updated during the project. Others will be maintained throughout the course of the project as living documents. When should they archive documents as historical records for future projects?

   A. Throughout the project
   B. Before the end of project planning
   C. During project closure
   D. Before the end of project executing

MASTERING THE PMP® EXAM [TOTAL PREP]

7. You're making sure the product of the project has been completed according to the project management plan. What part of the project management process are you in?

    A. Executing
    B. Closing
    C. Monitoring and controlling
    D. Planning

8. Which of the following is in the correct order?

    A. Collect requirements; define acceptance criteria; final transition of product, service, or result
    B. Define project scope statement; create list of stakeholders; final transition of product, service, or result
    C. Create list of stakeholders; final transition of product, service, or result; close procurements
    D. Validated deliverables; define cost performance baseline; final transition of product, service, or result

9. Which activity would not occur during project administrative, legal, or financial closure?

    A. Closing control accounts with finance
    B. Closing team assignments; release
    C. Closing collection of lessons learned
    D. Closing contracts

10. If the project is terminated prior to completion, what technique or tool may be used to close the project?

    A. Administrative Closure
    B. Expert Judgment
    C. Contract Inspection and Remediation
    D. Close Project

Notes

Earned Value Management

I. You have just completed the 3th week out of a 12th week project, and have the following information:

   CPI = 0.96
   SPI = 0.89
   AC = $125,000

   Calculate the following values assuming the original budget may still be achievable, and you are expecting to work at the budgeted rate going forward. Assume also that all work and spending are evenly divided through- out the duration of the project.

   i. EV =
   ii. PV =
   iii. BAC =
   iv. EAC =
   v. ETC =
   vi. VAC =
   vii. TCPI =

Given a project with the following characteristics, answer the following questions:

- You are the project manager of a project to build fancy birdhouses.
- You are to build two birdhouses a month for 12 months.
- Each birdhouse is planned to cost $100.
- Your project is scheduled to last for 12 months.
- It is the beginning of month 10.
- You have built 20 birdhouses and your CPI is 0.9091.

MASTERING THE PMP® EXAM [TOTAL PREP]

1. How is the project performing?
    A. Over budget and ahead of schedule
    B. Under budget and ahead of schedule
    C. Over budget and behind schedule
    D. Under budget and behind schedule.

2. What is the actual cost of the project right now?
    A. $1800
    B. $2000
    C. $2200
    D. $2400

3. If the COST variance experienced so far in the project will continue, how much more money will it take to complete the project?
    A. $400
    B. $440
    C. $2800
    D. $2840

4. If the variance experienced so far were to stop, what is the project's estimate at completion?
    A. $2400
    B. $2440
    C. $2600
    D. $2800

5. What is the project's TCPI using the project's budget at completion?
    A. .5
    B. 1
    C. 1.5
    D. 2

6. Senior management wants to the percentage of the project that is complete. What should you report?

    A. 75%

    B. 83%

    C. 92%

    D. 95%

7. Imagine if instead of 10 months and costing $2200, the project was in month three and costing $4000. What formula might you use for BAC?

    A. $\frac{(BAC-EV)}{(CPI \times SPI)} + AC$

    B. New bottom-up estimate

    C. AC + new ETC

    D. AC + BAC − EV

Notes

Critical Path Exercise

1. Draw a network diagram based on the data listed in the table below.

Task	Predecessor	Duration
1	none	13 weeks
2	1	6 weeks
3	2	6 weeks
4	1	8 weeks
5	2, 4	10 weeks
6	3, 5	9 weeks

2. What are the paths based on the network diagram?
3. What is the duration of each path based on the network diagram?
4. What is the critical path based on the network diagram?
5. What is the early start, early finish, late start, late finish and float for each activity based on the network diagram?
6. Which path represents the least schedule risk based on the network diagram?
7. If the duration for activity B changes to 9 weeks, what is the impact to the project?
8. Based on the previous change, identify options to reduce the project duration.

MASTERING THE PMP® EXAM [TOTAL PREP]

Process Matrix Exercise

Complete the matrix with the process groups, knowledge areas and processes.

Process Matrix | **6th Edition**

MASTERING THE PMP® EXAM [TOTAL PREP]

Inside each process box, write the project document outputs (some may have more than one)

Identify Stakeholder	Collect Requirements	Estimate Activity Duration & Estimate Costs	Identify Risks	Control Costs
Develop Project Charter	Plan Quality Management	Direct & Manage Project Work	Define Scope	Perform Integrated Change Control
Sequence Activities	Plan Resource Management	Manage Project Knowledge	Define Activities	
Develop Schedule	Estimate Activity Resources	Manage Quality	Control Schedule	
Acquire Resources	Estimate Costs	Control Quality		

159

Notes

ADV Consultants
PMP® Workbook Answers
PMBOK Guide 6th Edition

Introduction

Matching

1. Project
2. Operations
3. Program
4. Portfolio
5. Stakeholder
6. Sponsor
7. Project Life Cycle
8. Project Management

Fill in the Blanks

1. Project Team
2. Project Management Office
3. Functional Organization
4. Project Expeditor
5. Project Coordinator
6. Projectized
7. Balanced Matrix
8. Project Manager
9. Functional Manager

Memorization

1. Enterprise Environmental Factors
2. Develop Project Charter
3. Integration Management
4. Tool
5. Output

6. Planning
7. Monitor & Control
8. Closing
9. Executing
10. Organizational Assets
11. Work Performance Information

Matching

1. Integration Management
2. Scope Management
3. Schedule Management
4. Resource Management
5. Quality Management
6. Cost Management
7. Communication Management
8. Stakeholder Management
9. Risk Management
10. Procurement Management

Crossword Puzzles

Across

2. Project Documents
5. Project Management Plan
6. Feedback

Down

1. Work Performance Data
3. Expert Judgment
4. Change Request

Fill in the Blanks

1a. Supportive

1b. Controlling

1c. Directive

2a. Functional

2b. Projectized

2c. Balance Matrix

3a. Project Coordinator

3b Project Expeditor

4a. Scope

4b. Schedule

4c. Budget

Multiple Choice Questions

1. C
2. A
3. C
4. B
5. A
6. C
7. A
8. C
9. A
10. B

Notes

MASTERING THE PMP® EXAM [TOTAL PREP]

Project Management Roles and Responsibilities

Fill-in the Blanks

1a. Leadership
1b. Technical Project Management
1c: Strategic and Business Management
2. Laissez-Faire
3. Transactional
4. Servant Leader
5. Transformational
6. Charismatic
7. Interactional

Matching

1. Positional
2. Referent
3. Expert
4. Reward-Oriented
5. Punitive or Coercive
6. Authentic
7. Social
8. Managerial
9. Emotional
10. Intellectual

Initiating

Matching

1. Business Case
2. Agreements
3. Assumption Log
4. Stakeholder Register
5. Project Charter
6. Develop Project Charter
7. Identify Stakeholders

Questions

1. **B.** – The project scope statement is created in project planning. All the other choices are addressed in project initiating.
2. **D.** – Operational work is work that sustains the business. It may or may not be done in the context of a project.
3. **A.** – Evaluating the effectiveness of risk responses and recommending changes and defect repair occur in project monitoring and controlling. Updates based on lessons learned are done in project closing. High-level acceptance criteria are determined in project initiating.
4. **C.** – Assembly line in a car manufacturing is an example of a business process that is ongoing and repetitive.
5. **B.** – The project manager does not have the option of selecting stakeholders. Stakeholders are people or organizations whose interests may be positively or negatively impacted by the project or its product, as well as anyone who can exert positive or negative influence over the project. All stakeholders must be identified and managed to ensure project success.
6. **C.** – Assumptions are first identified in initiating, although additional assumptions may come to light as the project progresses. They are analyzed in project planning, and they are reviewed for validity and managed throughout the project.

MASTERING THE PMP® EXAM [TOTAL PREP]

7. **B.** – The project manager should be assigned during project initiating.

8. **A.** – When identifying new stakeholders, it's important to add them to the list of stakeholders and determine what they will mean for the project. As these 600 stakeholders will likely have no influence or authority over the project, the best strategy may be to keep them informed. It is not practical to interview all 600 stakeholders, so this is not the best answer. Getting the stakeholders to sign off on requirements is also not correct, as it's unlikely you'd need sign-off from all of them, and sign-off of the requirements would already have been done anyway. The stakeholder engagement assessment matrix is useful for evaluating the difference between the current and desired levels of stakeholder engagement It should already have been created and used in the planning that was done. It would be appropriate to add the new stakeholders to the matrix, to analyze their stakeholders' engagement, but that is not an answer choice. In addition to the stakeholder engagement plan, the requirements, communications, and risk management plans will also be impacted by this discovery.

9. **A.** – The opportunity cost is simply the value of the project(s) the organization did not select.

10. **A.** – Interrelationships between stakeholders, their communication requirements, and level of engagement are determined in the Plan Stakeholder Engagement process and documented in the stakeholder engagement plan. The stakeholder register includes stakeholders' roles, major requirements, levels of influence, and classifications.

Notes

MASTERING THE PMP® EXAM [TOTAL PREP]

Planning

Matching

1. Project Statement of Work
2. Cost Budget
3. Requirements Documentation
4. WBS Dictionary
5. Activity Cost Estimates
6. Project Scope Statement
7. Requirements Management Plan

Matching

1. Activity list
2. WBS
3. Activity Cost Estimates
4. Project Scope Statement
5. Cost Baseline
6. Source Selection Criteria

Fill-in the Blanks

1. Create WBS
2. Decomposition
3. Lead
4. Lag
5. Analogous Estimating
6. Parametric Estimating
7. Bottom up Estimating
8. Resource Smoothing
9. Funding Limit Reconciliation
10. Cost of Quality

Fill-in the blanks

1a. Fast track

1b. Crushing

2. Work Package

3. Escalate, Avoid, Mitigate, Accept, Transfer

4. Escalate, Exploit, Share, Enhance, Accept

5. Offer, acceptance, competent parties who have the legal capacity to contract, lawful subject matter, mutuality of obligation, consideration

6a. Firm Fixed Price

6b. Cost Reimbursable

6c. Time & Material

7a. Push

7b. Pull

7c. Interactive

8a. Verbal

8b. Formal Written

8c. Informal Written

Questions

1. a.

2. b.

Fill in the Story

1. Develop Project Management Plan
2. Project Management Plan
3. Collect Requirements
4. Brainstorming
5. Bench Marking
6. Interviews
7. Focus Groups
8. Questionnaire and Surveys
9. Requirement Traceability Matrix
10. Define Scope
11. Project Scope Statement
12. Decomposition
13. WBS
14. WBS Dictionary
15. Activity list
16. Define Activity
17. Sequence Activities
18. Network Diagram
19. Estimate Activity Duration
20. Develop Schedule
21. Schedule Baseline
22. Cost Management Plan
23. Estimate Cost
24. Parametric Estimating
25. Analogous Estimating
26. Bottom Estimating
27. Determine Budget
28. Cost Baseline
29. Quality Management Plan
30. Quality Metrics
31. Process Improvement Plan
32. Plan Resource Management
33. Resource Management Plan
34. Team Charter
35. Estimate Activity Resources
36. Plan Communication Management
37. Risk Management Plan
38. Identify Risks
39. Risk Register
40. Perform Qualitative Analysis
41. Probability and Risk Matrix
42. Watch list
43. Perform Quantative Analysis
44. Expected Monetary Value
45. Make or buy analysis
46. Procurement Management Plan
47. Stakeholder Engagement Plan

Notes

Put in Order

Place the processes in the box into the correct planning order.

1. Develop Project Management Plan
2. Plan Scope Management
3. Collect Requirements
4. Define Scope
5. Create WBS
6. Plan Schedule Management
7. Define Activities
8. Sequence Activities
9. Estimate Activity Durations
10. Develop Schedule
11. Plan Cost Management
12. Estimate Costs
13. Determine Budget
14. Plan Quality Management
15. Plan Resource Management
16. Estimate Activity Resources
17. Plan Communications Management
18. Plan Risk Management
19. Identify Risks
20. Perform Qualitative Risk Analysis
21. Perform Quantitative Risk Analysis
22. Plan Risk Responses
23. Plan Procurement Management
24. Plan Stakeholder Engagement

Matching

1. Benchmarking
2. Check lists
3. Check Sheets
4. Interviews
5. Focus Groups
6. Market Research
7. Statistical Sampling
8. Questionnaires and Surveys
9. Brainstorming

MASTERING THE PMP® EXAM [TOTAL PREP]

Questions

1. **C.** There are only two choices related to scheduling: critical path method and precedence diagramming. Precedence diagramming is a diagramming technique that deals with the relationship between activities, not schedule flexibility. The project manager is analyzing the critical path.

2. **B.** The key words here are "potential problems." They are looking into the future and, therefore must be in Plan Quality Management

3. **A.** The Plan Communications Management process involves identifying communication requirements, including the identification of any communication preferences.

4. **D.** This question is asking you about the process of project management. Estimate Resources Durations are completed during Resource Management. Collect Requirements is done before the WBS. Network Diagram is done during Sequence Activities. The next thing to do is Develop Schedule.

5. **D.** Activity cost estimates, the resource management plan, and the project schedule are inputs to the Determine Budget process, which takes place in project planning.

6. **D.** The project charter is created during project initiating. Completing work packages is done during project executing. Validating scope and performing integrated change control are done during project monitoring and controlling. Starting to create management plans is the best choice, as it is part of project planning.

7. **A.** SWOT analysis involves assessing strengths and weaknesses within the project, looking for opportunities, and threats that could result from them. This technique is used when identifying project risks.

8. **D.** The resource histogram shows the resources used per time period. The responsibility assignment matrix shows the tasks the resources are assigned too. The resource management plan describes when resources will be brought onto and taken off the project, and how team members should communicate with the project manager, would provide the most benefit for this project.

9. **B.** The milestone list and risk register are project documents. Lessons learned are an organizational process asset. Baselines are components of the PMP.

10. **D.** The requirements traceability matrix is a grid that links product requirements from their origin to the deliverables that satisfy them. Typical attributes used in the requirements traceability matrix may include a unique identifier, a textual description of the requirement, the rationale for inclusion, owner, source, priority, version, current status, and status date.

Executing

Matching

1. Deliverable
2. Issue log
3. Change Request
4. Lessons Learned Document

Fill in the Story

1. Direct and Manage Project Work
2. Project Management Plan
3. Preventive
4. Corrective action
5. Work Performance Data
6. Manage Knowledge
7. Lessons Learned
8. Manage Quality
9. Process Improvement Plan
10. Acquire Resources
11. Tuckman Ladder
12. Team Performance Assessments
13. Manage Team
14. Problem Solving/Collaborating
15. Manage Communications
16. Communication Reports
17. Conduct Procurement
18. Bidder Conference
19. Select Sellers
20. Implement Risk Responses
21. Manage Engagement

Notes

MASTERING THE PMP® EXAM [TOTAL PREP]

Questions

1. **D.** – First, determine under which knowledge area the described activities fall. With reference to sponsors and stakeholders, you may guess that it is Stakeholder Management. However, the activities of collection, creation, distribution, storage, and monitoring project information fall under Communications Management. Next, determine what process group is related to these activities. Is it Planning or Monitoring & Controlling? No, the task is not to develop the communication models in Planning, nor is the task to identify if the planned communications artifacts and activities have had the desired effect. Instead, the current activities are mostly collection, creation and distribution and delivery, which take place while executing the work of the project. An important clue is that you are distributing work performance reports, which is an output of the Direct and Manage Project Work process in the Integration knowledge area, in the Executing process group. Therefore, the correct answer is that these activities fall under Manage Communications.

2. **A.** – The scenario implies you are performing the Manage Stakeholder Engagement process which is concerned with communicating and working with stakeholders to meet their needs, address issues, and foster involvement. One of the inputs to this process is the project management plan which provides guidance regarding stakeholder communications, risk management, change management, and stakeholder engagement. Specifically, the stakeholder engagement plan contains information on how to manage stakeholder expectations thus helping to determine how to engage the stakeholders effectively.

3. **D.** – A resource calendar identifies the working days, shifts, start and end of normal business hours, weekends, and public holidays when each specific resource is available. Information on which resources are potentially available during a planned activity period is used for estimating resource utilization. Resource calendars also specify when and for how long identified team and physical resources will be available during the project. Of the available choices the resource calendars, provides the best source of information for the project manager about the availability of a team member to perform project work.

4. **C.** – The team charter is a document that records the team values, agreements, and operating guidelines, as well as establishing clear expectations regarding acceptable behavior by project team members. The team charter may be updated to reflect changes to the agreed-upon team operating guidelines that result from team development. Of the available options, discussing the issue with the team and updating the team charter accordingly is the best course of action in this situation.

5. **D.** – The performing organization's human resource management policies represent one of the enterprise environmental factors which may influence the Develop Team process. Before taking any action regarding the team member's employment, you should first review the enterprise environmental factors, specifically, the human resource management policies that specify hiring and termination procedures.

6. **C.** – To communicate effectively, project managers must employ their interpersonal and team skills which are also among the tools and techniques of this process. In the question described, the project team has determined that there are no viable solutions to avoid the missing deadline. This inevitable outcome must be communicated to the customer, even if the conversation is uncomfortable.

7. **B.** – The objective of Conduct Procurements is to select a seller and award a contract. Therefore, Select Sellers is the output. Bidder conferences are a tool and technique the project manager can utilize.

8. **A.** – The objective of Manage Knowledge is using existing knowledge and creating new knowledge to achieve the project objectives and contribute to organizational learning. Therefore, the lesson learned document will be used throughout the project to document what worked well and what could be improved in the future. The document will be part of OPA's to use on future projects.

9. **A.** – Manage Stakeholder Engagement is where the project manager will communicate and work with stakeholders to meet their needs and expectations, address issues and foster appropriate stakeholder involvement.

10. **A.** – When internal resources are not available you have little choice except to go to an external source, following the change process. Answer-B seems reasonable but his peers most likely report to the same program manager, who should know if there are available resources. Answer-C is not a good idea as it was probably not budgeted as a long-term solution. Answer-D seems practical but could damage his relationship with his program manager who is empowered and has already made decisions.

Monitoring & Controlling

Matching

1. Alternate Analysis
2. Earned Value Analysis
3. Iteration Burndown Charts
4. Performance Reviews
5. Reserve Analysis
6. Root Cause Analysis
7. Stakeholder Analysis
8. Trend Analysis
9. Variance Analysis
10. Technical Performance Analysis

Notes

Fill in the story

1. Monitor and Control Project Work
2. Work Performance Information
3. Performed Integrated Change Control
4. Change Request
5. Validate Scope
6. Inspection
7. Accepted Deliverable
8. Control Schedule
9. Schedule Forecasts
10. Project Funding Requirements
11. Control Costs
12. Work Performance Information
13. Control Scope
14. Correctness
15. Verified Deliverables
16. Control Procurements
17. Claims Admiration
18. Inspection
19. Audits
20. Closed Procurements
21. Monitor Risk
22. Technical Performance
23. Reserve Analysis
24. Monitor Communications
25. Interpersonal
26. Team Skills
27. Monitor Stakeholder Engagement

Questions

1. **C.** – Other project constraints such as scope, cost, quality, risk, resources, and/or customer satisfaction should be evaluated. Once these are evaluated, the integrated change control board should be initiated.

2. **D.** – The formula is CV = EV – AC. Therefore, CV = 350 – 400, or CV = -50. PV is not a factor in this calculation.

3. **B.** – The project manager should perform a value analysis, looking for less costly ways to complete the work.

4. **A.** – A breach of contract occurs when part of the contract is not performed. In this example, the breach is the lack of monthly acceptance tests.

5. **A.** – Estimate at completion means the total cost of the project at completion, based on current information.

6. **B.** – Although the deliverable meets the contractual requirements, it is best to bring the problem to the customer's attention so an option that does no harm can be found.

7. **B.** – Validate Scope is a process of project monitoring and controlling.

8. **D.** – The project manager must evaluate before deciding. Even if dealing with the problem is not within the project manager's authority, it is still her job to do the evaluation before taking any other action.

9. **B.** – Even though the measurement was not identified in planning, the project manager would still have to investigate the variance and determine if it is important. The project manager is in project monitoring and controlling.

10. **D.** – Making sure project processes were followed, the right resources were used, and that all work was done could point out root causes of decreased cost. You cannot find ways to increase the result until after the root cause analysis.

Closing

Fill in the Story

1. Accepted
2. Lessons Learned
3. Staff Management Plan

Questions

1. **A.**
2. **B.** – Performance measures are determined earlier in the project so they can be used to measure progress during the project.
3. **B.** – Performance reporting in administrative closure communicates the success of the team.
4. **B.** – The project charter is created in initiating. The project management plan and risk management plan are outputs of project planning. Project records, including the charter and all management plans, are archived in the Close Project or Phase process.
5. **C.** – First, you need to document the reasons the customer will not sign off on acceptance. Once you understand the issues, you can work to resolve them.
6. **C.** – Documents are collected throughout the project. They are archived during the Close Project or Phase process.
7. **B.** – Notice that the work described in this question is product verification, not scope validation. The Validate Scope process occurs in project monitoring and controlling. Product verification is done in the Close Project or Phase process.
8. **A.** – Answer A is the best choice of them all for placing things in the correct order. The Final Transition of the deliverable is an output of Close Project or Phase, which is the last process done in any project.
9. **D.** – Contract closure is performed during the process Control Procurements, not Close Projects or Phase. All other closings listed here are valid during this final process to complete.

Notes

MASTERING THE PMP® EXAM [TOTAL PREP]

10. **B.** – The PMBOK Guide lists 3 common tools for this process, and Expert Judgment is the only correct tool listed in the answers. The other 2 are Meetings and Data Analysis. Administrative closure procedures are methodologies that are performed with the use of expert judgment. However, the name given for the tool or technique is the familiar one: Expert Judgment.

Earned Value Management

I.i. $EV = CPI = \frac{EV}{AC}$

Therefore:

EV = CPI × AC

EV = 0.96 × $125,000

EV = $120,000

Because we know CPI and AC from the facts of the question, use the CPI formula and solve for the missing value (EV) by multiplying the CPI by AC. This should be your first step, because knowing EV will be critical to answering the remaining questions.

I.ii. $PV = SPI = \frac{EV}{PV}$

Therefore:

$PV = \frac{EV}{SPV}$

$PV = \frac{\$120,000}{0.89}$

PV = $134,831.46

Now that we have the value for EV, we can plug in the other known values to the SPI formula to solve for PV. Here, we are given the SPI in the question and we now know EV, so we simply plug those in and solve for the missing PV value by dividing EV ($120,000) by our SPI (0.89).

MASTERING THE PMP® EXAM [TOTAL PREP]

I.iii. BAC = PV × 4

BAC = $134,831.46 × 4

BAC = $539,325.84

Here we must determine BAC, which is our original total budget. The first step is to know where we are in time, and the facts tell us we are ¼ of the way done. It may be tempting to just take AC and multiply by 4 to get the total BAC, but don't take the bait. Remember, AC is what we actually spent, not necessarily what we planned to spend. We need to know what we planned to spend in total, so we look to the current PV because there are no other clues given. Because we know the work is evenly spread across the 12 weeks, we know that our production rate should be linear, and therefore the PV for the next 3 periods should each match that of the current period. Thus, we multiply our PV at the ¼ mark by 4 and get our BAC of $539,325.84. This will tell us the total value of work we planned to achieve, using the spend rate we built into our budget.

I.iv. $EAC = \frac{BAC}{CPI}$

$= \frac{\$539{,}235.84}{0.96}$

$= \$561{,}797.75$

Things get a lot easier now, since we have the key values we need (EV, PV, BAC and AC) to perform any earned value equation. Because spending is expected to continue at the current rate (meaning variances are typical), we use the BAC/CPI formula to get our Estimate at Completion forecast (which is what we now believe we will spend in total to complete the project).

I.v. ETC = EAC − AC

ETC = $561,797.75 − $125,000

ETC = $436,797.75

ETC tells us what we will spend from this point forward, to complete the project. The ETC formula is always the same (EAC-AC) regardless of the circumstances (we already accounted for those circumstances when we calculated EAC). Thus, we subtract our Actual Costs of $125,000 from our Estimate at Completion of $561,797.75, and we know we will need to spend another $436,797.75 to complete the project (assuming spending continues at the current rate).

I.vi. VAC = BAC − EAC

VAC = $539,325.84 − $561,797.75

VAC = −$22,471.91

Variance at Completion (VAC) tells us the difference between our EAC (updated total budget forecast now that we are doing the work) and our BAC (original budget we established during planning). This formula is always the same regardless of the circumstances (we already accounted for those circumstances when we calculated EAC). The VAC of −$22,471.91 tells us we expect to spend $22,471.91 over our original budget to complete the project.

I.vii.
$$TCPI = \frac{BAC - EV}{BAC - AC}$$

$$TCPI = \frac{\$539{,}325.84 - \$120{,}000.00}{\$539{,}325.84 - \$125{,}000.00}$$

$$TCPI = \frac{\$419{,}325.84}{\$414{,}325.84}$$

TCPI = 1.01

The 'To Complete Performance Index' (TCPI) tells us how efficient we must be with costs moving forward in order to finish within our original budget (BAC). This tells us that we need to get $1.01 in value from every $1 spent for the remaining 9 weeks of the project to make up for our current shortfall in cost efficiency and deliver the project on budget.

Notes

MASTERING THE PMP® EXAM [TOTAL PREP]

1. **A. Over budget & ahead of schedule.** – The problem tells you that your CPI is 0.9091, and we know that CPI = EV/AC. Applying that, a CPI less than 1 means that we aren't getting enough value for each dollar that we put into our project, so it is over budget. However, the project is ahead of schedule because we have built 20 birdhouses and after 9 months, we had expected to build only 2 birdhouses per month * 9 months = 18 birdhouses.

2. **C. $2200.** – If you weren't quite sure whether the project was over budget in the last question, you can use this problem to strengthen your knowledge. In this problem, we need to determine the AC. In the body of the problem, you are given the CPI and can determine the EV, so you can use the CPI formula to back out the AC. EV = 20 birdhouse and $100 per birdhouse = $2000.
   - CPI = EV/AC
   - 0.9091 = 2000/AC, multiply both sides by AC
   - AC (.9091) = 2000, divide both sides by 0.9091
   - AC = 2200

3. **B. $440.** –First, use the context of the problem to determine that you need the ETC when a variance exists, and it is continuing. Based on that information, we know to use ETC = BAC/CPI – AC. We already know the CPI from the problem and AC from the solution to #2, so let's find BAC.
   - BAC = 2 birdhouses per month * 12 months * $100 per birdhouse
   - BAC = $2400
   - ETC = BAC/CPI – AC
   - ETC = 2400/0.9091 – 2200
   - ETC = 440

4. **C – $2600.** – A few of the EMV questions you encounter on the PMP exam will be straightforward. This question is asking you for the EAC if a variance that was encountered on a project is expected to stop, so use EAC = AC + BAC – EV.
   - EAC = 2200 + 2400 – 2000
   - EAC = $2600

MASTERING THE PMP® EXAM [TOTAL PREP]

This problem wouldn't be so straightforward if it were standing on its own. Based on our answers to the previous three questions, we already knew AC, BAC, and EV. The real PMP doesn't have answers that build upon each other, so your steps to solving this problem on its own would be less straightforward. Instead you would first determine which equation to use, then calculate AC using the CPI (as in question #2), then BAC as in question #3, then EV as in question #2.

5. **D – 2.** – Fortunately, PMI must tell you which TCPI formula to use. This one says use BAC, so

$$TCPI = \frac{BAC - EV}{BAC - AC}$$

$$= \frac{2400 - 2000}{2400 - 2200}$$

$$= \frac{400}{200} = 2$$

6. **B – 83%.** – If you have the percent complete formula in front of you, then this problem is easy. Just plug EV & BAC into (EV/BAC) *100%, and you're all set. If you got this problem wrong, then review this article (https://magoosh.com/pmp/pmp-topics-ev-pv-ac/) on EV, PV, and AC.

7. **C – AC + new ETC.** – It may be tempting to pick A but remember that the EAC formula is for when a project is past due. If you find that your estimates are wildly wrong at the beginning of a project, it is best to develop a bottom-up estimate to complete and then add that to your actual costs.

Critical Path Exercise

1. The paths based on the network diagram: (1236, 1256, 1456)

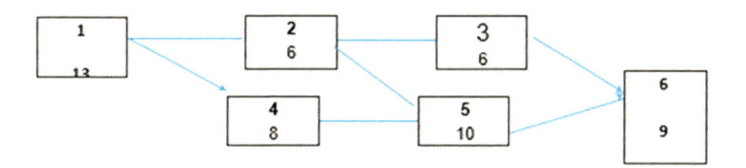

   ```
   [1]      [2]      [3]
    13       6        6
                             [6]
            [4]      [5]      9
             8        10
   ```

2. 1236 = 34 weeks (13 + 6 + 6 + 9)

   1256 = 38 weeks (13 + 6 + 10 + 9)

   1456 = 40 weeks (13 + 8 + 10 + 9)

3. The critical path based on the network diagram: 1456, with a duration of 40 weeks (13 + 8 + 10 + 9)

4.

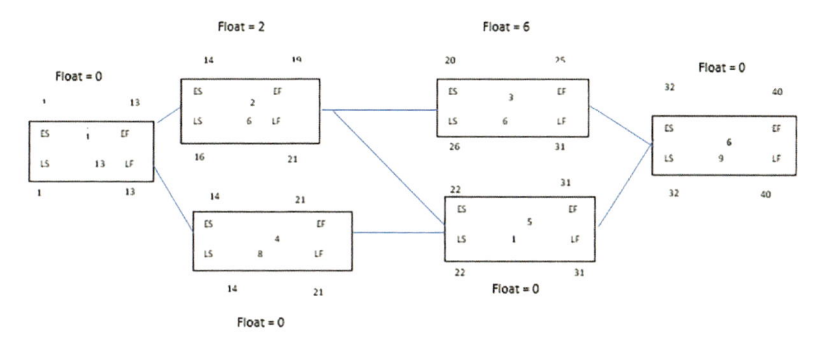

   ```
                  Float = 2              Float = 6
              14         19           20         25
   Float = 0   ES    EF              ES    EF              Float = 0
       13       2                     3                 32         40
    ES    EF   LS  6  LF            LS  6  LF         ES         EF
   LS  13  LF    16        21        26        31      LS    6    LF
    1         13                                       32    9    40
                  14         21        22        31
                   ES    EF            ES    EF
                       4                    5
                   LS    LF            LS    LF
                   LS  8  LF            1
                  14         21        22        31
                  Float = 0            Float = 0
   ```

5. The path with the least schedule risk based on the network diagram: 1236, with a duration of 34 weeks

   (13 + 6 + 6 + 9)

6. If the duration for activity 2 changes to 9 weeks, the impact to the project is that there is a new critical path:

   1236 = 37 (13 + 9 + 6 + 9)

   1256 = 41 (13 + 9 + 10 + 9) – New Critical Path

   1456 = 40 (13 + 8 + 10 + 9)

Notes

7. All options to reduce the schedule must be analyzed with respect to overall project impacts, and those options include:
8. "Crashing," which involves adding resources to a project activity to make it finish sooner. Here, either internal or external resources can be added to Activity E on the critical path. Crashing almost always increases costs, however. The activity on the critical path with the lowest crashing cost should be considered first.
    - Utilizing the same resource on a critical path activity but having that person work overtime. This could be considered a form of crashing because you are using more resource hours and costs will rise.
    - Adding a more skilled resource (if possible) on a critical path activity to reduce time. This is also a form of crashing in that you are adding greater resources to finish sooner.
    - "Fast tracking," which involves changing the sequence of activities so that some activities run in parallel, instead of sequentially. Fast tracking assumes that the dependencies between the activities are discretionary. Fast tracking almost always increases the risk of rework.
    - Lowering the quality standards, but only if approved by the stakeholders.

MASTERING THE PMP® EXAM [TOTAL PREP]

Process Matrix Exercise

Process Matrix	6th Edition					
	Initiating	Planning	Executing	Monitoring & Controlling	Closing
Integration Management	Develop Project Charter	Develop Project Management Plan	Direct & Manage Project Work	Monitor & Control Project Work	Close Project or Phase
			Manage Project Knowledge	Perform Integrated Change Control	
Scope Management		Plan Scope Management		Validate Scope	
		Collect Requirements		Control Scope	
		Define Scope			
		Create WBS			
Schedule Management		Plan Schedule Management		Control Schedule	
		Define Activities			
		Sequence Activities			
		Estimate Activity Durations			
		Develop Schedule			
Cost Management		Plan Cost Management		Control Costs	
		Estimate Costs			
		Determine Budget			
Quality Management		Plan Quality Management	Manage Quality	Control Quality	

Resource Management		Plan Resource Management	Acquire Resources	Control Resources
		Estimate Activity Resources	Develop Team	
			Manage Team	
Communications Management		Plan Communications Management	Manage Communications	Monitor Communications
Risk Management		Plan Risk Management	Implement Risk Responses	Monitor Risks
		Identify Risks		
		Perform Qualitative Risk Analysis		
		Perform Quantitative Risk Analysis		
		Plan Risk Responses		
Procurement Management		Plan Procurement Management	Conduct Procurements	Control Procurements
Stakeholder Management	Identify Stakeholders	Plan Stakeholder Engagement	Manage Stakeholder Engagement	Monitor Stakeholder Engagement

Notes

Identify Stakeholder **Stakeholder Register**	Collect Requirements **Requirements Documentation/ RTM**	Estimate Activity Duration & Estimate Costs **Basis of Estimate/ Duration of Estimates**	Identify Risks **Risk Register/ Risk Report**	Control Costs **Cost Forecasts**
Develop Project Charter **Project Charter**	Plan Quality Management **Quality Metrics**	Direct & Manage Project Work **Issue Log**	Define Scope **Project Scope Statement**	Perform Integrated Change Control **Change Log**
Sequence Activities **Network Diagram**	Plan Resource Management **Team Charter**	Manage Project Knowledge **Lessons Learned Register**	Define Activities **Activity List/ Activity Attributes/ Milestone List**	
Develop Schedule **Schedule Data/ Project Schedule/ Project Calendars**	Estimate Activity Resources **Resource Requirements/ Resource Breakdown Structure**	Manage Quality **Test and Evaluation Documents/ Quality Report**	Control Schedule **Schedule Forecasts**	
Acquire Resources **Project Team Assignments/ Physical Resource Assignments/ Resource Calendar**	Estimate Costs **Cost Estimates**	Control Quality **Quality Control Measurements**		

CPSIA information can be obtained at www.ICGtesting.com
Printed in the USA
BVIW121146250419
546532BV00008B/79